From Battersea

through

"Beaucaillou"

Reminiscences of a life in the wine trade from the 1970s through to the 1990s, and the characters and personalities I met on that journey

W. H. Cullen (Fulham) . Independent Bulk Wine Shippers . W. H. Cullen (Battersea) . André Simon Wines . Walter S. Siegel Ltd

- ◊ -

◊ Ramillies ◊
•
Design Press

- ◊ -

British Library Cataloguing in Publication Data:

A catalogue record of this book is available from the British Library

ISBN: 978-1-8381732-2-7

E-mail: briangatesuk@gmail.com

Formatting by Ramillies Design Press

DEDICATION

To Ben, Beckie, Sue, Tom and my dear Nina

CONTENTS

INTRODUCTION

The original thoughts behind producing this book were for my family. Having had a relative, my grandfather, who served in the Royal Navy and whose service career we knew very little about I pieced together the fascinating story of his naval life. It turned out that what he experienced, in both World Wars was remarkable, and in our eyes, he is not unnaturally a hero.

During his lifetime he chose not to say much about his experiences of war, which was natural given what he had experienced, but having found out so much more now on what he encountered, we perhaps wish we had prompted more conversations on the subject for posterity.

It occurred to me that whilst we all live a life unless something is either said or written on it, it is lost to time.

For our children, the chance to understand what we ourselves experienced in our working lives, as they themselves travel through life and face their own challenges, may or may not be of interest to them. But, there are parallels in every generation, and perhaps reflecting on our own thoughts and feelings at that given point in time, and sharing this with them, shows that they too are not alone on their journey.

The experience itself has been an intense but fulfilling one, recalling memories and the sensations you felt at a given time prompts a myriad of emotions.

To write about my past in the wine trade would be of little use if not applying one simple criterion, to tell the truth. Whilst this may seem obvious it is easy to see how either embellishment or distortion can creep into such projects. For those with inflated egos you can see the attraction, but to make any work meaningful it must be honest and reflect the true experience.

Wine as a subject in this country has often been associated in the past with class or elitism. I was reminded of this recently by a book written by Evelyn Waugh *Wine in Peace and War*. His musings and pontifications on the subject render the subject as if it were almost incomprehensible to the ordinary man or woman – be he working or middle class. Taking on an almost mystical air of elitist knowledge, understood by only the top echelons of society, it would appear that the book is both ludicrous and highly amusing in its nonsense!

My entry into the wine trade would owe little to either connections or privilege, but a real desire to learn about a subject that fascinated me.

In this respect, I of course met many people on the journey. Here again, I wanted their memory not to be forgotten, people that made you laugh or admire, or those whose personalities shone through and acted as an inspiration. With every uplifting moment, there was naturally a counterpoint that is part of life's journey.

I hope the words that follow bring some of those I met who are no longer with us back once more and the places or scenarios that are long gone reimagined once again in the mind's eye.

Brian Gates

London, 2023

ACKNOWLEDGEMENTS

I should like to thank the following for their encouragement and help. Trisha Furnell, Susan Gates, Tom Gates, Steve Langdon, Maureen Plummer, Nina Roussinova, and of course Ben for his patience and help.

I would also like to thank David Blaze for the chance to reignite memories after such a long period and to * Mike Peterson of breweriana.org.uk for his knowledge on Guinness collectables, and a long-time supporter in my Tuckers Malting days.

My particular thanks go to the following for their time and contributions in remembering someone who left us far too soon.

Thank you, Nigel Blundell, Paul Boutinot, Jane Hunt MW, Robert Joseph, Katie Macaulay, Angela Muir MW, Francis Murray, Jancis Robinson MW, and Paul Tholen MW. All comments are those of the individual contributors.

Particular thanks go to Robert Joseph for 'rallying the troops' and to Francis Murray for his further efforts.

Lastly to William and Hilary Rogers, and in particular to William for sharing his memories with me.

FULHAM ROAD – THE BEGINNING

My first ever experience of work was thanks to my mother, Pat, who worked for W.H. Cullen's at the wine head office in Battersea.

Through her daily dealings in the office, with the paperwork and telephone, she was well acquainted with the managers of the company's 90 plus wine shops, and it transpired that the manager of one of the shops, in Fulham Road SW6, required some help from a young lad and she suggested me. I was excited about the prospect of earning a little bit of pocket money for myself. A source of independence!

I was around 13 years of age at the time and had never really visited this part of London before, although only over the bridge from where I lived in Battersea, Fulham Road was very different.

I remember my very first day of arriving at the shop. As I entered (no doubt very nervous, and shy) I saw a gentleman behind the counter wearing a brown warehouse coat and glasses with a fixed forward gaze, and arms out stretched confidently attached to the countertop (who in my eyes at least) with his stance, seemed to be the archetypal manager. On asking if he was, it turned out he wasn't and was the delivery driver for the shop. He called through the door to the back of the shop and the manager came rushing out, a very different individual indeed, Mr. Ivan Pascoe.

He did not appear as I imagined at all, wearing just his normal clothes, smart but casual, extremely tall it seemed to me then, and svelte-like. He was indeed built for speed, as I would soon see. He was very engaging and we discussed the hours I would work, Tuesday and Thursday evenings after school for two hours, and Saturday mornings from 9 till 1pm. Ivan will be covered in a separate chapter.

W. H. Cullen's was perhaps more renowned then for their delicatessen side of the business than their wine and the combined shop was located on the corner of Gilston and Fulham Road. The wine shop was a smaller separate entity with its own entrance on the Gilston Road side, whilst the food store entrance was on Fulham Road.

The shop address was 182/184 Fulham Road and the combined shop had been specifically rebuilt by the architect's Gale, Heath and Sneath for W. H. Cullen with the building line set back, between the years 1936 and 1937.

The shop as it appears today, with just one entrance, unlike the Cullen period when the wine entrance was on the right in Gilston Road, in a position close to the street lamp.

Internally the wine shop was very much in the tradition of the day. Furnished with dark wood shelving and panelling with some elegant mouldings, and over a foot in depth for each cubby hole. These covered the entire side of the shop length to

12

perhaps some nine feet in height. The shelving extended in a similar fashion behind the counter. Although dark, it all had a touch of serious elegance about it, and when fully stocked looked impressive.

The stock rooms for the shops were at the very back of the store, to the right for the wine side and to the left for the food side. These were reached by a narrow passage which would only allow one person to pass at any one time (more on this later). There was a small office just behind the food shop to the left (which I only ever ventured into once) and another stock room for food to the right, behind the wine shop. In this area, more of the staff would congregate.

The delicatessen being bigger had more staff of course, with Mr. Southernwood the manager, a younger assistant, who seemed very confident, and a lad perhaps three years older than me called David. Of the ladies that worked there Mrs. Mary Measures I remember as being warm and friendly, and another lady whose name I cannot recall, equally so.

I remember that on my first Saturday I was unsure whether to bring lunch so purchased from a bakery in Fulham Road (for the one and only time!) a Rum Baba, It was a big mistake and tasted dreadful!

THE WORKING ROUTINE

I soon learnt that speed and accuracy were the essences of the job as the wine shop was extremely busy at times. If I arrived after school in the evening I was soon off at full speed attempting to restock the shelves. Mr. Pasco would give me the heads up and I was off like a ferret! I enjoyed the challenge very much.

In those days companies such as Cullen's bottled their own Guinness. Being in the one-pint returnable bottles and in heavy 'W. H. Cullen' embossed green plastic crates (which I would encounter again later in the trade!) the shop sold high volumes of it, so it constantly needed replenishing on the shelves.

Bass beer bottles were also returnable then, and behind the counter, a large deep heavy duty wicker basket about four feet by two with a metal tray in the bottom would have the returnable Guinness and Bass bottles tossed into it. In no time at all these would turn acetic and vinegar permeated from it with green mould settling on the remnants of the stale beer in the tray. It all needed to be sorted through and the empties crated up, it was all part of the job, and I thought nothing of it.

Schweppes soda water then was also in the heavy-duty glass syphons with the white spouts and in old (some ancient…) wooden crates (six to a case) that were heavy and unwieldy, with loose rusty hinged lids that rarely sat squarely on stacking.

The spirits, wines, liqueurs and beers I soon began to learn by name and sight and worked as hard as I could to do a good job.

One of the strange things about youth is how you interact with others. Returning to the stock rooms, which were accessed by the narrow passage, a sort of informal traffic light system seemed to take place.

If David from the delicatessen side was heading up or down with a box or crate I would naturally give way and slip into an available gap somehow, and he did likewise for me. But for all the years we worked there we never spoke to each other, a nod of recognition as we passed to and fro but never a conversation. Yes we were both busy of course and I was younger than him, but we both just plied on with the work.

I wore a blue warehouse coat I seem to remember and my most trusty piece of equipment, as it were, was my cleaning cloth in my pocket, the rule being that every bottle that went on to the shop floor must be clean in presentation. It became second nature, so much so that I often did it automatically without thinking. I took a great deal of pride in getting the shop faced up correctly, labels all facing the right way, and the work being appreciated.

On the food side, Mr. Southernwood too was an interesting character, he was very old school, never smiled, and dominated the delicatessen side of things. Again I think I only ever spoke to him once, ever, otherwise, it was a deferential smile and nod.

He was very prim and military-like in his precision. I remember the cardboard boxes when empty in the food stock room had to be flattened, tidied and strung up correctly to his satisfaction. He would stand stone-faced and watch like a hawk whoever was given the solemn task (either his assistant or David). He would slowly lean forward onto his toes, and rock back and forth in this controlled manner with his hands clasped behind his back ready to pounce! Not doing it to his high standards was simply not an option!

I found it fascinating to watch out of the corner of my eye and never forgot his foot manoeuvres!

Delivery day for the wine shop from the head office in Battersea was on a Thursday, and I would be extremely busy re-stocking the shelves and putting all the remainder of the stock away from the delivery in the stock room in the evening, or on a Saturday when I had more time if it could not be completed. I enjoyed working on my own doing this, getting it all organised in the best way possible given the limited space.

I was fascinated by the assortment of brands, the vibrant labels and packaging, and the number of different lines the shop held, although I knew very little about the products of course.

I would spend nearly three happy years working at the shop, but an interest in military aircraft, something I had had from an early age, led me to apply to Hawker Siddeley Aviation in Kingston as an engineer. I was accepted, and whilst I thought this would be my future direction this turned out not to be the case.

I had not forgotten my experience in the wine shop and on leaving Hawker's asked Mr. Pascoe whether it would be possible to be employed in the shop on a full-time basis. I knew this was a big ask, but he enquired and thankfully it was, and so my career in the wine trade in the true sense was about to begin, although in terms of direction then I was unsure which route it would take of course.

IVAN PASCOE

Going back to that very first day when I arrived at the shop (and wrongly assumed the driver was the manager!) when meeting Ivan Pascoe, the real manager, I was immediately taken by his manner.

He was very different to the atypical manager of the day and had a certain lively spirit and informality in the antipodean way (being that he was originally from New Zealand) that made him engaging.

He was open, easy to approach and always took time to answer your question (with an encouraging and enquiring "Go on..." in his lilting accent) no matter how simple it may have been. It was such a contrast to being at school, he treated you in an adult manner, and I respected and appreciated that enormously. Not that he wasn't authoritative and had his own distinctive way of dealing with people and customers. I wanted to work hard for him.

I always addressed him as Mr. Pasco, but in later years when we met of course, as Ivan.

He was also popular with the delicatessen staff too who probably appreciated his bohemian nature, and also of course extremely knowledgeable about wine, having learnt this over many years, with a very good palate.

His physical manner of working was sometimes a source of worry as he worked at breakneck speed. If a customer enquired about an item that was in the stock room at the back he would make an immediate beeline for it, almost crashing into other members of staff, then with either a sudden halt or weaving in and out, always managed somehow to avoid a disaster! He was extremely hard working and made the shop a great success.

I always remember his dealings with customers. Being that the shop was on the Fulham Road it had its fair share of those that felt slightly superior or pretentious, but such was his knowledge that he quickly put these people in their place, in his relaxed but no-nonsense approach.

Often customers would come in and ask for "a cheap bottle of wine" to which his calm measured response was "we only sell inexpensive wine sir/madam, not cheap".

He had a set pattern or routine and probably highlighted 3 or 4 wines to a customer who asked for advice, and always based on his tastings of the product. This he would do with a slight gaze into the distance as he recited his patter, always engaging and professional, but obviously, it became repetitive. Sometimes he would have to do this routine several times a day, and it would not always result in a sale of course, but more often than not he was successful and customers respected his judgement.

Amongst the many questions I no doubt asked over the period I worked there, one in particular I remember was when we were selling Chateau Latour 1967.

What fascinated me about this wine then was that when I asked Mr. Pascoe why it was selling for £15 a bottle (at 1976 prices, and considerably more than any other red wine in the shop then) he informed me it was one of the "1er Grand Cru Classé wines, but that the year was not a particularly good one". This really intrigued me that a wine from a poorer vintage could command such a price, and I wanted to learn more.

Another memory I have from that period is when the area manager, a Mr. Bluett a friendly gentleman, asked Mr. Pasco whether I could help him remove some stock from the Cullen's wine shop on the Grays Inn Road which was closing down. Ivan had known the manager well, who had recently died, and knew he had some stocks of fine claret which could be transferred to our shop for sale.

For me, a chance to do something a little different appealed and we headed over to the shop. Being similar to ours in terms of design I remember it did have a cellar underneath, which I gingerly went down into, and in the far corner spied a beautifully old ornate scrolled Victorian till which still shone even having been there for many years. It seemed incredibly large, and I remember wondering how heavy it was, so giving it a hefty nudge realised it was as solid as a rock and going nowhere!

Once we had loaded up the van we headed back to Fulham Road and unloaded the boxes. We had wine bins for laying down stock just behind the till and I brought the bottles up ready to lay them in the bins.

Handling the bottles carefully I began to give them a gentle clean with my trusty cloth, only to hear an outcry from Mr. Pascoe "No no don't do that, you mustn't remove the dust!" I was slightly dumbfounded, as this was the first time I had heard this, and going against protocol, or so I thought.

Mr. Pascoe then took the time to explain that connoisseurs of fine wine would look to see the dust running along the length of the bottle as an indication that it had been laid down correctly in a bin to age with the label uppermost.

This also triggered a surge of fascination in my mind, so here was something that you must NOT clean!

The problem was, in trying to be efficient I had already cleaned half a dozen bottles, but then hit upon the idea of picking up a pinch worth of dust between my two fingers and sprinkling it slowly along the length of the bottle, and gently blowing it off.

To my surprise, and relief, in comparing it with the bottles that had not yet been cleaned you could hardly see any difference. The whole experience, rather than being upsetting in any way, really fired my enthusiasm to learn more, and I am eternally grateful to Ivan Pascoe's intervention!

One gripe I do remember Mr. Pascoe had was the great British public's obsession with talking about the weather! The poor man would have to take part in this meaningless conversation umpteenth times in a day, and as I would listen in I could see his face glaze over and form into that distant stare as he answered a customer yet again on this pointless drivel. He understood it was all part of the sale and had to be endured, but clearly not part of New Zealand culture!

As my interest in wine developed further, I remember my first purchase in the shop and starting from what was definitely the lower order, I purchased a bottle of Cullens 'Culvin Vin Rouge'. This Mr. Pascoe assured me was a good starting point, so as to draw comparison with other wines as I would move up the price scale.

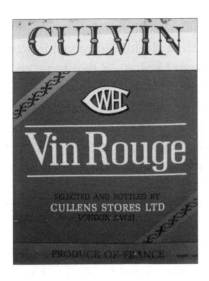

From the bottom upward! The first wine I purchased at Fulham Road, the label very much of its time.

It was also during this period that I would meet James Rogers for the first time. James had joined Cullen's in 1971 and at this point was running the wine division.

One day as I was filling up stock on the shop floor James came in to see Mr. Pascoe on a shop visit. He seemed a very lively, confident, cheerful individual, and Ivan introduced me. Whether this was as "Pat's son" (as James knew my mother at head office) I cannot recall, but I do remember him saying that I was learning from "one of the best managers" which was a nice endorsement of Ivan's talents, and something I wholeheartedly agreed with.

One aspect of Cullen's which I think has never been fully appreciated was that not only were they to become one of the leading chains in introducing wines from many areas from around the world and innovative, but at this time (the early 1970s, and tapping into the CAMRA interest) they were leading the way on the traditional ale front too.

They had a range of regional ales from independent brewers, which other retailers were simply not stocking, from Ruddles (brewed in Rutland then!) King & Barnes in Horsham, Theakston's from Masham at that time, and perhaps the most unlikely to see in the south of England, Samuel Smith's from Tadcaster (not to be confused with its much larger next door neighbour John Smith's, which has long since lost its independence), amongst others. The Samuel Smith brewery in particular I have always felt was a particular coup, and at that point in time, their ales were truly distinctive in flavour and style.

I would have another encounter with this company, but in a different capacity, further on in the story.

Some trivia of interest perhaps is that being that the shop was on the Fulham Road I do remember some celebrities would call in. Claire Bloom the actress was charming, and I do recall Leonard Rossiter (a great wine enthusiast) cupping his hands around his face one day and looking through the glass door of the shop, although not coming in. David Langton the actor from the popular period drama Upstairs Downstairs was another who called in fairly regularly.

One of the strangest memories from that time was of a young lady who called in who I have only recently realised who she was, and where I had seen her before!

I remember she came up to me in the shop and asked me for an inexpensive bottle of wine. She appeared very glamourous, polite and friendly and although I was young I recommended a very popular budget wine of the time Sidi Larbi from Morocco, going at a bargain price of 99p a bottle! This she said was ideal and happily purchased the wine.

On watching The Beatles *A Hard day's Night* recently I now know that this was Edina Ronay who was the 'face of youth' in the film going by the fictional name of Susan Campy. Coincidentally, David Langton also had a part in the film.

I spent a very happy year working for Mr. Pascoe, but still unsure then of my future direction it was time to leave. I had learnt a great deal from him, and he truly was a wonderful person to work for, generous with his knowledge, kindly and encouraging, and a remarkable person who I remember with great affection.

During my time with Ivan, he could see my interest in both wine and beer, and a gift I have always treasured from him was a can of Guinness he gave me. This was no ordinary can, it was part of a show card display unit once used in the shop's window, and as such had never held any beer! Today it is a rare item which originated in 1957 and was produced at the Park Royal Brewery in London. My thanks go to Mike Peterson* on this point with his extensive knowledge.

The next year would be spent at college after which it was time once again to consider my future. I had never forgotten my experience in wine and it interested me greatly, although my knowledge then was rudimentary. Then, by chance or fate, an advertisement in a newspaper decided the next direction I would take. Wine once more, but in a very different capacity!

INDEPENDENT BULK WINE SHIPPERS

On replying to the advertisement I was invited along for an interview and made my way to Lambeth. The company was situated underneath a railway arch at Carlisle Lane, and on entering I found the office over on the left-hand side of the arch.

Here I met David Blaze the manager in his white lab coat and we sat down to talk. Although I was young (around 19) I think it was probably the fact that I had some limited wine experience that perhaps swayed it at the interview, and he offered me the position. Quite what the job entailed was not clear, but I would soon find out one aspect of it!

As the company name suggests 'IBWS' dealt predominantly in bulk wine and with an adjoining arch had a variety of fibreglass bulk wine tanks of various capacities.

To say that the interior was not pleasant would be an understatement. The arches were not lined so water would work its way down from the roof hugging the walls, and green slime hung down from the tops of the arches, with dark mould patches in many areas. It was constantly damp, and wellington boots were the only possible footwear in such an environment.

There was metal racking for storing boxed wine on pallets, but the damp would soon seep into the cardboard, so moving stock quickly out was the best option. There was a small bottling line in the second arch.

It was however ideally suited to bulk wine storage, keeping a cool temperature through summer, but could be bitterly cold in the winter as often the main shutter would stay up at the front of the arch.

There was a courtyard in front of the arches and a prefabricated style administrative office was to the left.

Apart from David Blaze I only remember one other member of staff at the beginning called Ronnie. He was a few years older than me and always held an affable smile, and worked in the bulk wine section.

On day one I soon discovered what the job involved. Whilst I enjoyed hard work of course I had not been expecting this, and it was a far cry from working in the shop.

There were a number of large heavy-duty plastic barrel drums which were perhaps 4 feet in height by 2 feet in circumference and held over 40 gallons of wine in each. These had all been left out in the yard waiting to be cleaned, and it was my job to do it.

I was shown the process which involved using a large metal key to undo the plastic stopper on the top of the drum and half filling it with water. Then a large dose of liquid sulphur was poured in, enough to knock your head back violently with just one sniff!

Unwieldy to handle, you would then have to roll the drum around the yard back and forth sloshing the mixture around for as long as it took to remove any trace of acetic acid from the previous filling. Periodically you would stand them upright and sniff through the bung area, and if there was still a trace, carry on.

I have often felt that you were given this job on your first day just to see whether you were going to last the course. It was very physical and would have come as a shock to many, and whilst initially, I did not enjoy it, I soon became used to it, and after a while thought nothing of it and developed my own technique.

What the drums were for was for filling with a Spanish red used in the recipe for Homepride 'Cook in Sauce'. The drums once filled with wine would then also be sulphured to the hilt to preserve it!

SETTLING IN

Slowly I settled in and various other jobs came my way. I showed a fair amount of aptitude, and over time other jobs with more responsibility were passed to me. I was very quiet and happy to get on with the work, and during lunch would sit silently observing others. It was a friendly atmosphere.

You soon got a feel of how things worked. The delivery driver Albert seemed to be one of those people who always had his finger on the pulse, and would relay snippets from the managerial office in the courtyard. I only ever remember going into that office itself once in all the time I was there.

The owner of the company was Ron Haze, a diminutive figure with black-rimmed glasses, who always seemed to be bustling around. He was a true salesman, a character, and had obviously done well as it was clear that trade was on the increase within the business. He was always pleasant to the staff and counted loyalty as important in return. I believe the company itself was connected to Robert Porter, of Porter & Laker who dealt in bulk wine in a big way in the trade at that time.

I also remember Dave ('Senior'), an elderly gentleman then who had been a mentor to David Blaze in the past, who was no-nonsense but pleasant, with a military bearing. They had both worked together at Mike Hewlett's and David Blaze had invited him to come and work with him at IBWS as the company was getting busier.

I always remember that during lunch a sort of ritual would be played out. A polypin of 'Vin de Liqueur' would be on the bench (a fortified wine from the south of France) and available on tap. Dave 'Senior', as if always spying on it for the first time, would amble up to it and award himself a generous medium-sized goblet full. He truly enjoyed it, extolling its virtues you could tell by his manner that it had hit the mark, so much so that another glass worth was called for, and quite rightly then, he was truly satisfied!

Not long after I joined a lady called Jean started also, Albert had found her the job, and he had a soft spot for her I used to think. Another character who joined at some point during this period was Tosh. It is strange that you can work with so many people but never get to know their surnames, but in this case, I never knew Tosh's real Christian name either, he was simply 'Tosh', but more on him a little later...

As mentioned earlier there was also a bottling line on-site, and when bottling from the tanks the wine was passed through a sterile filtering machine. Whilst some machinery was relatively new, others were definitely not. An old stalwart of the wine trade was the Purdy Labelling Machine, a marvel of the inventive mind it had so many moving parts your brain boggled at its movements! Its sole purpose was to put a label on a bottle, but it had so many foibles that on occasion this seemed like the last thing it was capable of!

The arches in Carlisle Lane.

The IBWS arches were closer to the apex with Royal Street, but on the building of the Eurostar stations at Waterloo in the early 1990s, the yard areas have disappeared and been replaced by supporting structures for the new lines above. The arches themselves may go back to the mid-1800s.

This picture of a young David Blaze (on ladder) was taken at the Lyons Wine Cellars at the Hop Exchange, Southwark. The other gentleman below is unknown. The tank containing Meursault is interesting as these were exactly the same at IBWS. This shows 550 gallons but there were also 250 and 1100.

It was operated by a foot trestle, and one day while I adjusted the holdall to fit a particular bottle size I unscrewed the bolt underneath, which was the usual practice. I was on one knee and then with a slight distraction, I realised I had made a big mistake; I had not turned the machine off. My knee then pushed down on the foot trestle and my hand then became trapped in the machine. My hand was pinned down fast between the metal label plates and the bottle itself. Then blood immediately spouted out from the hand, and I looked on in a sort of stunned disbelief as my blood shot out like a fountain. Eventually, it was released but was bleeding heavily, so a trip to St Thomas's Hospital not far away was in order. I had learnt my lesson.

The wine imported by IBWS reflected very much the tastes of the time. Apart from the bulk French and Spanish wines, which played a big part in the company's success, they also imported bottles from Germany. I remember a contract for Browns Restaurants being an important one with constant bottlings taking place, plus several other regular customers as demand increased. One wine I do recall was Credo, a Cyprus sherry destined to be an alter wine. Anything was possible!

What was clear is that the company was doing well and growing. This in turn meant that Albert the delivery driver was also increasingly busy and he employed extra drivers on the back of this. Another piece of relative trivia is that one day during lunch the door opened and a young black gentleman asked around "Has anybody seen Albert? It's just that I have joined this band and I won't be able to work for him anymore". This turned out to be Joe Leeway of the Thompson Twins.

I worked well with David Blaze; he was very efficient, hardworking, and with a calm nature. He would pass on further jobs of responsibility to me and eventually, on the knowledge that Ronnie was due to leave, asked me if I would like to run the bulk wine section. I remember talking to him and Dave 'Senior' in the car one day and asking if there were any books on the subject to help me learn more. They both jointly commented it was the sort of job that you learnt through experience being passed on by others, which they would do.

Toward the end of 1978 news came through that the company could be on the move. It had outgrown the arches at Lambeth, and the conditions were less than satisfactory, but what shape this new move would take we did not know.

It had transpired that the old wine company of Mason Cattley & Co. Ltd, which was based then at 2-6 Pennington Street in Wapping, had been implicated in a wine fraud and exposed by a national newspaper. IBWS would therefore take over the company and move to this new address.

All the existing staff was asked if they would like to move to the new site, and although we had misgivings about the distance involved in terms of travel, I think nearly everyone agreed to go. We knew very little about the area other than it was in the East End and near the old Wapping docks.

As usual, Albert seemed to know more than most, and I can remember him saying that the new company would be known as 'Kopke'. When hearing this I remember thinking how odd the name sounded, and I was unaware then of the historical significance of the name. Whilst it was not a change of company name all future labels on whatever wine bottled at the new address would carry the name of C.N. Kopke & Co Ltd.

I soon learnt that travel to the new location was indeed not that simple. Living in Battersea you could travel by bus as far as London Bridge Station and from there, at that time, there were no transport links to Wapping. This then would mean a walk up Tooley Street, then over Tower Bridge, down the Highway, and eventually down Virginia Street before arriving at Pennington Street. It was a fair trek, which was also dependent on whether Tower Bridge was raised, which occasionally it was, and adding further delays!

Travelling up Tooley Street I remember the large offices of Teltscher Brothers at numbers 60-66 who imported at that time the extremely popular brand of Lutomer Riesling.

Arriving at Pennington Street for the first time the large dock walls and the sheer size of the warehouses were foreboding. The area had a sense of melancholy about it, no doubt brought on by the fact that the docks were no longer the hive of activity they once were. I did however feel a sense of pride that I was to work in an area that was once so central to the wine and spirit trade, this was the last vestiges of an industry that had almost disappeared altogether from this area. Firms of all sizes storing and bottling the wines landed at the docks would have filled this area once, but no more.

The warehouse we were to work in was originally built in 1882 by Gooch and Cousens Wool Merchants, a thriving and important industry in its day, and was five stories in height, with a central yard within. By comparison to where we had been in Lambeth, it seemed a big change.

Pennington Street today. The large dock walls still exist opposite the Mason Cattley site, although the similar wall that ran up Virginia Street has been demolished.

With the exterior largely unchanged Mason Cattley occupied the first floor and
basement area as shown on the left here. Breezers Hill on the right with its
cobbled pavement, a sense of the past still exists.

MASON CATTLEY & Co Ltd - AND THE TAKEOVER

My first impression of our new location at Pennington Street was that it was an
impressive set-up. The cellars, just below street level, appeared well organised and I
remember the eye-catching site of the descending sizes of measuring wine jugs
hanging from one of the beams.

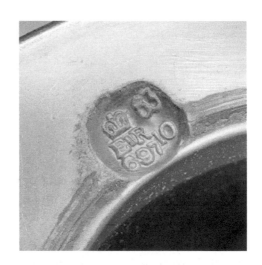

The smallest in the collection of tin measures, the original stamped Pint jug from the Mason Cattley cellar that hung from the beam.

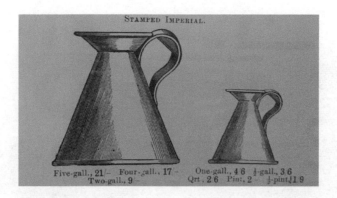

STAMPED IMPERIAL.

Five-gall., 21/- Four-gall., 17 -   One-gall., 4 6 ½-gall., 3 6
Two-gall., 9 -   Qrt., 2 6 Pint, 2 - ½-pint,J1 9

From the Farrow & Jackson catalogue for 1898. It shows the descending sizes of the measuring jugs.

I recall there were two large wooden hooped vats beautifully made, which were sold off to Merrydown Cider makers I think. I always thought it was such a great shame, they had real character.

The cellar itself was divided into a number of large chambers, each of which carried heavy-duty burgundy red painted iron doors with a large round bolt lock that drew across. This may well have gone back to the period when it was a wool warehouse and designed to contain a fire within the chamber. Either way, it was eerily quiet in each chamber, and the doors remained open until the end of the working day for forklift and general access.

The bottling line too was considerably larger than what we had previously, and the expansion in warehouse-size compared to the arches was considerable.

One of the more difficult aspects I remember was meeting with the Mason Cattley cellar staff. Clearly, they were not overjoyed at the takeover, and some would cold shoulder you, especially an elderly man who was their supervisor, but the younger ones seemed more engaging. It was not a comfortable mix though, and as will be seen things would change, but we tried to focus on the work.

The cellars were very orderly in terms of stock, with pallets of wine neatly stored away, clean and organised. The quality corrugated boxes on the pallet were printed with 'Mason Cattley & Co Ltd' and the company logo and looked professional.

I remember on one of those early days whilst walking through the warehouse coming across a gentleman writing down a list of stock on a pad whilst standing by a pallet. We pleasantly exchanged hellos, and I, being simply a young warehouse staff member, and he being management, would have no further involvement, and in fact, I never saw him again.

This was however Paul Bohane, and the list he was taking was part of the stock that was due to be sold off to auction at either Christie's or Sotheby's and was the fraudulent wine that the company had bottled. He had been part of the deception.

THE WINE FRAUD

We had first heard about the fraud itself when the takeover had been announced back at IBWS in Lambeth and knew few details, other than the company had been exposed by a Daily Mirror reporter who was said to have been lurking down the end of Pennington Street! It all sounded very cloak and dagger, and a touch humorous to us younger staff.

The fraud itself was exposed in the Daily Mirror on the 13th October 1978 with the dramatically sinister heading 'At least two men knew the dark secrets hidden in the cellars of Mason Cattley and Co. Ltd., wine shippers'.

Wine fraud of any sort, of course, is not acceptable, and it would not be until 1981 before the case would come to trial. It is sad to think that a wine company which had had such a strong association with the old port house of C. N. Kopke should end in such a manner, but this was the case.

The Times newspaper reported on the 9th April 1981:

Five men fined for wine label fraud

Five men from a respectable firm of wine importers put false labels on bottles of inferior blended wine, the Central Criminal Court was told yesterday.

The men bought appellation contrôlée and declassified wines from the same area of France and blended them, Mr David Tudor-Price said for the prosecution. The wines were then given appellation contrôlée labels.

The five, from the Mason Cattley company, all admitted conspiring to contravene a section of the Trade Descriptions Act and conspiring to commit false accounting.

Paul Bohane, aged 46, company director, of Culverden Park, Tonbridge, Kent, his brother, Austin Bohane, aged 69, chairman and managing director, of Wadhurst, East Sussex, and Rex Mead, aged 66 sales director, of Thames Ditton, Surrey, were each fined a total of £500.

Ken Buttell, aged 51, sales manager, of Mitcham, Surrey, and James Morrison, aged 45, shipping manager and stock controller, of Colchester, Essex, were fined £100 each.

Richard Tooth, aged 60, the company's former accounts clerk, of Tattenham Corner, Epsom, Surrey, had denied one charge of conspiring to contravene a section of the Trade Descriptions Act. The prosecution offered no evidence and he was discharged.

New staff would also join at this time and a young man Eric (who resembled Al Green!) I remember I got on particularly well with, and a young lad Michael joined who was pleasant too. Jean's daughter later joined as well and she was a tough young woman, built for the physical work the cellar offered.

With Ronnie gone I was more than busy in the bulk wine area, from the tankers arriving with the wine, transferring the wine to the various areas of the cellar, filtration, fining, preparing for bottling, plus the thorough cleaning of tanks. David Blaze passed on his knowledge which was a great help of course.

One strange and less than perfect invention I remember that was used occasionally was filling half-filled tanks of wine with vast quantities of plastic balls. They were similar to a ping pong ball, but of tougher plastic, and maybe two and a half inches across in diameter. The theory was that as oxygen brought on a wine's deterioration these balls would fill the air space in the tank. As they did not sink they just accumulated on top of the wine, but you needed an awful lot of balls to fill say a half-empty 1100gallon tank! As can be imagined the work required in emptying the balls out of the tank once empty was hard going!

I also recall closer to Christmas being given a task that was considered to be a responsible one, and important to get right, of packing up bottles of port for the corporate customers. The wine had arrived from Portugal and been bottled at the lodge in Vila Nova de Gaia.

This was the first time I had come across Kopke Port and I remember the red dipped wax over the cork, stylised labels of the ruby and tawny, and the serious-looking nature of the vintage port labels making an impression on me. This coupled with the embossed bottles incorporating the Kopke trade mark on the wood ports made for products impressively packaged.

Something else also fascinated me; a small cupboard within the cellar, perhaps 10 feet in length by 6 feet, that housed all the Kopke labels used by Mason Cattley & Co Ltd. going back a long way and all were neatly stored. The designs for all manner of ports bottled by the company were there with their vibrant colours and intricate artwork. In the past, nearly all port wine was bottled in the UK.

A bottle of Kopke Quinta St. Luiz 1977 Vintage Port from my time at Pennington Street.

The bottling line (initially) was run by a member of staff who had been part of the Mason Cattley crew who clearly knew his job and got on well with us, but the underlining feelings of unease amongst other staff remained. Some staff from Mason Cattley just left of their own accord unhappy at the takeover.

Nevertheless, it was a busy time and the warehouse was a hive of activity and the company seemed to be doing well. On several occasions, I can remember working late as it was so busy, and on one occasion at least until 10pm, with David Blaze dropping us off at a point we could get transport home more conveniently.

There was also enough work for family members to come and work at IBWS during the summer holidays. My younger cousin Mark came to work there for two weeks during one such holiday. I remember him saying to me he had "no idea how hard I worked!" But, he too had to work hard through that period, and if your body wasn't used to the physical nature of it, it was tough. At the end of the first week, he was looking forward to his pay packet, but the company had forgotten to add him to the pay role. As we both headed home to Battersea I could see the utter dejection in his face, so I gave him my salary that week to lift his spirits.

The company had also gained a bit of a reputation it seemed at being good at relabelling wines for customers if required, and something I think Ron Haze the Managing Director actively pursued to keep additional work flowing in the cellar. One customer had been particularly happy with a job we did I seem to recall, but Mr. Haze clearly thought we were capable of bigger things!

A JOB TOO FAR

This bigger thing would take the form of relabelling litre bottles of Jameson Irish Whiskey which had a label unsuitable for the UK market, and we were to soak off labels from the entire stock and relabel it!

This was on a different scale as pallet loads of the whiskey arrived in the cellars and the job of removing the labels proved more than a challenge! To their credit (and I am sure Jameson's were well aware of this) the labels were never designed to come off and the glue had no intention of allowing such a thing! Any hope of soaking the label off cleanly was impossible so the only alternative was to scrape them off with knives or any other similar implements.

Some of those self-same heavy-duty wine drums that had welcomed me in the early days at IBWS were cut in half and used as water butts to soak the bottles in, and there were rows of them prepared in the cellar before we began the task of working on the labels. The problem was of course you could not have the water in the butts too hot, which meant it went cold quickly making your hands go numb and raw in the process. Water and glue were everywhere. The scraping never left a clean job and there were always stubborn remnants of glue in some form or another on the bottles. All the young members of staff would work away on this job when time permitted, but it was thankless work, to say the least. On top of this, the heavy bottles would sometimes break in the butts, which you could not always see in the water, so shards of glass were another hazard.

This was perhaps a job too far, and Ron Haze had underestimated the work involved. We did finish the job eventually but the relabelling was not good. No fault of ours of course just that the original label had no intention of leaving the bottle without a fight, and in this case, it had won!

TOSH & DAVE 'SENIOR'

One of the joys of working at IBWS was to see the interactions between Tosh and Dave 'Senior'. Tosh was very much an East End character, warm-hearted, wise and worldly with high values. Small in stature he sported a perfectly rotund stomach, which caused the buttons on his brown warehouse coat to strain, and wore glasses and a flat cap that never left his head. I would marvel at how he would talk and move a safety match between his lips from one side of his mouth to the other with his tongue, perfectly balanced and in constant motion, it went back and forth and never faltered!

Dave Senior however was very different with (as mentioned previously) a military bearing, very proper and exact, and lovely sharp humour. One of his favourite sayings, when David Blaze the manager would arrive, was "Stand by your beds!" Both these two gentlemen complimented each other perfectly, worlds apart in terms of backgrounds, but their mix of humour was a delight to watch. There was warmth and mutual respect, and they were so fun to be around.

Tosh of course not having any wine background would tend to be the butt of Dave Senior's jokes, but always with a sense of affection, and never unkind. It was like watching a perfectly matched double act.

I always remember Tosh standing with the Flogger (the wooden bat used to drive home a cork) giving the stopper corks in the bottles a hearty bash as they passed down the bottling line. Cries of "Woah Woah Woah!" would go up when there was a jam on the line, and good-humoured banter would start as to whom was the culprit! Anyone was game for a ribbing.

I recall on one occasion when it was Tosh's birthday being invited to his local pub to celebrate and we all headed off with him. It was an archetypical East End pub with pictures of boxers on the walls and seemed a bit unnerving to us, but he was clearly a popular local character and held in high respect, as did we.

There were of course other high jinks the younger staff would get up to. The temptation of the Lansing Bagnall forklift truck was something most of them wanted to drive. When all the bay doors in the warehouse were open it resembled an unofficial race track, and I can recall Eric on at least more than one occasion going at such speed on the bends that he was on two wheels! Health and Safety were not foremost in most youngsters' minds, but it does not bear thinking about if the forklift had rolled over.

I too had an encounter on the forklift. On one occasion where a ceiling was lower in the far end of the cellars, I lifted the cradle so high it hit the florescent tube above me and exploded into thousands of glass flakes like confetti! In a natural reaction, I had put my hands and arms over my head as protection as it exploded and had felt nothing, and thought all was well. As I sat there stunned what felt like an even distribution of blood as if in slow motion, began to run down the sides of my head. Front, sides, and back all had blood, and bizarrely, all seemed to be running down evenly at the same slow speed, it was a surreal moment. It was nobody's fault but mine of course, and I had felt no pain. I was taken to a hospital nearby where two young attractive nurses slowly began to remove the glass flakes with tweezers from my hair and head.

Another strange occurrence I remember, whilst working in a far chamber with David Blaze explaining a hand wine labelling job to me a gentleman came rushing toward us and clearly looked shocked, and bewildered. "Have you seen Ron Haze!" he asked, and David Blaze said he hadn't. The gentleman was John Fells.

MOUNTING PROBLEMS

After some time a problem hit the cellars which had a big impact – a wild yeast infection. At first, it was hard to understand the significance of this event, and as we were bottling large orders for customers the disturbing news came back that the wine was infected and had to be returned to the cellars. This meant opening and emptying all the bottles into a tank, sulphuring, re-filtering the wine again, and re-bottling into new bottles and re-labelling. Once this was done the wine was sent out again to the customer, and yet again it was infected and had to be returned. As can be imagined this created a lot of work, in effect, it was doubling or trebling a single job. Each time the wine was re-filtered and returned to the customer, more flavour was stripped from it.

We tried to deal with the yeast infection in the bulk wine cellar and I can recall us scrubbing away at the floors, walls and anything else that may have been causing it. It was a difficult time as you were chasing an unseen enemy as it were, and never sure if you were on top of it. In many instances, despite all our best efforts, we were not. This went on for some time and I do recall an expensive AC wine, I think it was a Puligny Montrachet fermenting away vigorously in a tank infected, and we were unable to do anything about it.

On one occasion, in sheer desperation, a senior member of management climbed a ladder to the top of a tank, removed the bung, and began to pour cases of perfectly good Vin de Liqueur into a Spanish Tarragona red wine that had been infected. It was a futile attempt that really only served to waste perfectly good fortified wine! The bulk wine was beyond help.

Before long customs officers were called into the cellars as hundreds of gallons of wine had to be poured down the drains. Although the company could recoup the duty, the loss of this whole event must have been high for the business, and over time the problem was slowly resolved.

It now appeared that changes were afoot, and the first redundancies were announced. This would involve the existing Mason Cattley staff. Ron Haze with his no-nonsense approach called the individual members into his office on the first floor and gave them the news. Some, as would be expected, did not take it well. I can remember him coming down to us on in the warehouse and saying "I am sick of people telling me they know their rights!"

He was also expecting trouble, namely **sabotage**, and told us to stand by the tanks in case they tried to open the valves in an attempt to destroy the stocks! As a group of four or five of the Mason Cattley staff moved through the warehouse, obviously disgruntled at having been giving their notices and complaining, they did not take any action and simply left the premises.

The offices for IBWS were on the top floor and a glass cabinet in the hallway held a selection of Kopke port wine artefacts, some beautifully crafted miniature pieces that were used to promote the port house. There was a model of a Barco Rabelo in full sail (the traditional boat used in the Douro to transport port casks down the river) plus miniature barrels and lovely traditional signage, all articulately made. It really did show the close link that Mason Cattley once had with the port house - who they in fact had owned from 1870 up until 1953.

The reduced staff now ploughed on and we were back to the old IBWS team as we had been in Lambeth, plus the few new members that had joined us. But, sadly, the redundancies continued and it was a very sad day to see Dave 'Senior' leave as well as Tosh. We were deeply saddened by this, and so were they.

Moving into 1980 the company felt more unstable and we were all unsure of what the future may hold. David Blaze continued to do his best in difficult circumstances until one day the remaining staff were offered redundancy. We could continue, but you sensed the company was in decline and things had become erratic as work had fallen off considerably, so I, Eric and Michael took redundancy.

It was a sad end to the dedicated IBWS team. The move to take over Mason Cattley had been a gamble but it had not been a success. I had spent two and a half years with the company and was grateful for the experience, and it had definitely fired my interest in Port Wine.

The company went into liquidation on the 25th May 1981.

W. H. CULLEN WINE DIVISION

Having left IBWS it was time to look for work once more. My mother at this point worked at W. H. Cullen's in the wine division at Battersea. She had in fact left the company at one point but asked a friend there, Tommy Lambert, if she could return. She had worked her way up from initially working on the Kalamazoo system processing orders with the plates, to the office itself where she dealt with many of the Cullen's shop managers. Mum was intelligent, quick, efficient, excellent at maths and extremely well organised. She was popular with the girls in the office and worked well with whoever the office manager may be.

I had never ever considered working at the head office, as simply my working world and my mother's seemed leagues apart, but one day a vacancy became available in the cellars. As I now had experience in the handling of bulk wine, treatment, and bottling I felt I may have something to offer, so it was arranged that I would go for an interview with Clive Bird the Warehouse Manager. But it was understood that if I was unsuitable, then so be it.

The history of the Cullen building at 142-144 Battersea Park Road is an interesting one. It was originally built for Propert's as their new blacking factory and they moved there from South Audley Street in the 1870s. Designed by the architect George Ashby Lean it had (and still has) an impressive Gothic stock-brick façade. Propert's remained at the site until the Second World War and it is not entirely clear when Cullen's moved there but I would imagine in the late 1950s or early 60s. It was sympathetically renovated by the architect Geddes Walker in the mid-1980s.

Internally the building was a labyrinth and warren, and much of this will be described in the pages to come.

Access to the warehouse was in Warriner Gardens at the back of the building (the front entrance at 142 was never used) and here a loading bay was situated where the Cullen lorries' would load and unload, and deliveries were taken in. Clive Bird's office seemed to be perched precariously to the left above the loading bay and reached by a well-worn stairway.

The old office was small and cramped, with notes and papers pinned to walls in all sorts of places, and paperwork all about, but here we sat down to talk about the position.

Clive Bird had not long taken over from George Creffield who had run the warehouse and staff in a disciplined manner for many years. He introduced innovations such as the roller track system to the warehouse (about 16 inches wide) which enabled stock to be pushed around the building when orders were being collated. This was a system used in the army which may be where Mr. Creffield got the idea from, and it ran like a train track.

I liked Clive Bird immediately; he was honest, down to earth and realistic. Not showy in any way he was steady with a sense of humour and the interview seemed to go quite well. He appreciated that I had some experience and that I would be of help. The job would not just be confined to the bulk bottling room but all aspects of the wine warehouse as required, but he could tell that I was interested in learning more about wine. He offered me the position and then explained how much the salary would be. I then thanked him but refused the position on the grounds that the salary was too poor! Instead of being affronted by my reply, he agreed with me, so much so that he would go to the managing director immediately and inform him of my response!

I was unsure how this might play out, but I had been honest, and he would inform me in a few days' time of their response.

ROPERT'S CELEBRATED STANDARD BLACKING.
[B.BEDDOW & SONS, PROPRIETORS]   POLISHING PASTE.
BATTERSEA PARK ROAD,   IMPROVED KID REVIVER.
ESTABLISHED 1835 AT SOUTH AUDLEY ST LONDON.   PARISIAN GLOSS.

The architect's impression of the new Propert's blacking factory.

The two sections of the warehouse behind the main frontage shown here were used for wine storage during Cullen's time. The rear entrance in Warriner Gardens has a gate shown here. The small property at the back with the spire was for the night-watchmen/supervisor. It was demolished during George Creffield's time to allow easier access for the Cullen lorries.

After a few days had passed I heard from Clive Bird regarding the position and they offered a more realistic wage which I accepted.

I was unsure what to expect when I started, but the one thing that struck me immediately was just how antiquated much of the building and machinery was. In some ways, this had an old-world charm, whilst in others; it was desperately in need of some investment.

The frontage of the building as it appears today, with similarities to the architect's drawing. The Propert's signage has been emblazoned once more whilst the architect George Ashby Lean's foundation stone is in place on one side, and Geddes Walker architects who did the renovation on the other.

The internal layout of the building was fascinating.

The front of the building on the top floor had the offices and tasting room, but the warehouse was all around. The roller track system extended outside the offices too, so you had to skip over them back and forth as you walked from one area to another. Should you misjudge your footing you could ruin your shoes, so more of a problem for the ladies in the offices! Vast stocks of boxed wines were stored on this floor, all of which had to be handballed into place. This floor was also home to the bulk wine and bottling plant.

On the floor above this in the rafters was storage for slower moving lines such as liqueurs and miniatures, also with the roller track. I remember the antiquated steep wooden steps were worn almost polished flat on the edges and slippery from the bodies that had gone up and down them since the 1870s. You did not so much walk down them but slid down!

On the ground floor boxed wines of every country were stored along with beers, crates and more, and the roller track was here too. Some straight sections of the track about 6 feet in length were not fixed to the floor but movable and used for deliveries, which will be explained later.

Here was the loading bay too, and as the lorries backed into the raised concrete bay, which covered three walls of the yard, it allowed them to position themselves to take on the stocks for delivery. A large fire shutter, with a door for access, would come down in front of the bay at the day's end.

Below this in the basement were the low ceilinged cellars, with intriguing nooks and crannies. Here wines, such as clarets, burgundies, vintage ports, and other fine wines were stored. There were many iron bins for laying down wines, and a steady temperature was maintained here throughout the year.

An old lift perhaps 8 feet by 6 was at one end of the warehouse, which I remember was unnervingly slow and somehow you never felt you could trust it!

All the floors were connected by steep angled old wooden slat belt conveyors, which trundled at one speed as the goods made their journey to whatever level was required.

For the person taking the goods off at the top of the conveyor it could be hazardous, as the slats would wrap under and return, as it was a constant conveyor. Misjudging removing a box could lead to your arm getting dragged underneath with dire consequences. You were often on your own, and if you thought this was about to happen you quickly had to reach for the bulbous red stop button. The conveyors had seen better days and really should have been replaced long before. But, this really was the nature of the place, improvements were needed.

THE HIERARCHY

It was clear that things had remained unchanged here for many years, and it was very staid. There was almost a sad acceptance of the surroundings around them and routines and behaviour were firmly entrenched.

The warehouse staff I suppose must have numbered around 10 men and at 11am a whistle was blown for the tea break. As if to compound this feeling of rigidity, this meant a trip up the black-painted fire escape to the tea room, which resembled a chain gang, as the men tramped slowly up the stairs in the time-honoured fashion. I remember doing this in the early weeks and the sense of melancholy that filled the air as you pounded up the stairs.

Once in the room itself at one end to the left, an elderly lady stood behind a large tea urn, which puffed steam periodically, and there were old tables and chairs in the middle, with further chairs against the walls around the perimeter.

You then lined up in turn to get your tea, the hierarchy being the older staff going first, and once you had yours you carefully tried to find a place to sit which did not 'belong' to someone else. I recall sitting in a chair around the room's perimeter and scanning the other faces around me to try and gauge their personalities. You of course had some younger ones who were more ebullient, others cheeky, and some who just wanted to sit quietly and read a paper.

I remember one older gentleman was sitting alone at a table with his arms and elbows pinned rigid in a triangular fashion, and his fingers clasped tightly in front of his mouth with his chin resting on them occasionally. He just stared with a fixed expression at the door. The message from him was unequivocal; he did not want to interact with anyone. You could tell he had probably been working there for years and was waiting for the day when he would finally leave forever.

You sensed it was all much oppressed. I recall one day on the lower floor of the warehouse using a very basic toilet area, only to be told I was not allowed to use it in future, it was purely for the supervisory staff.

The design of the warehouse did not allow for the use of forklifts, and something I always remember was the delivery from the Samuel Smith's brewery flatbed lorry from Tadcaster. The roller system that had been introduced would now come into use, but this time those straight sections which were movable played their part. As the lorry was too large to back in it parked across the main entrance in Warriner Gardens, to which the straight sections were joined together in a long line one by one. As can be imagined this required a lot of sections as the distance from the lorry to the delivery bay must have been in the region of 60 feet! What was also essential of course was to make sure there was enough of an angle to allow the Samuel Smith's crates to travel down the sections, so all sorts of boxes or crates would be used to prop it up!

A section of the roller track system as used here by the US army, and at Cullen's.

Once this set-up was in place the unloading would begin. Some of the crates would travel down at such a speed that for the poor person waiting at the bottom it was like a projectile! Removing them into the warehouse was hard going, and your fingers could get caught as the rigid crates would snap at your fingers as others crashed into them. As more and more crates were put on the roller sections to try and speed things up so a jam would form. It was far from perfect and many bottles of fine beer were smashed in the process. I recall on one occasion a Samuel Smith's driver saying to me "do you have a forklift?" to which of course the answer was no, and he none too pleased, as his journey back to Tadcaster in Yorkshire would be a late one.

Wine tankers would also be pumped out from lorries positioned in Warriner Gardens. Mounting the top of the lorry a large 5-foot stainless steel lance pipe would be placed into the top hatch and from here pumped up to the bulk wine store. The pipe was unwieldy to handle, and you had to be careful on top of the lorry as the pump could give the pipe a kick, and could knock you off!

THE BOTTLING ROOM

Although I worked in nearly every area of the warehouse the main section I would work in of course would be the bottling room, and here three of us Gus, Bob and myself would get on with the work in hand. The room itself was set almost central within the warehouse so no windows or natural light.

In the past nearly all the wines imported by Cullen's would have been in cask, so the bottling line at that time would have been in constant use, but not located at Battersea. Cullen's then had the facilities at Waterloo Arches, known as the Bottling Stores; where, as well as wine beers such as Guinness, were also bottled. But, as trends changed more wine was coming in bottled at source, so the bottling line was moved to the Battersea site, and when I joined in 1980 the Waterloo Arches had closed. Nevertheless, the bottling line at Battersea was nearly always operating.

As for the line itself in Battersea, once again this was an antiquated affair. Some three large fibreglass tanks at the back of the room, along with perhaps some eight smaller 550-gallon sizes packed closer together were arranged on heavy wooden sleeper supports. The wines from the tanks would then pass through the filtering machine to the bottling line.

The machinery here comprised of a bottling machine (circa 1950 or 60s) with its circular head with 12 syphons coming of it, which when the bottles were filled were put on an old metal circular rotatable table, which was swung around by hand so

50

that they would meet the next person in the chain who would be on the corking machine. This vintage bit of kit would have a spring-loaded bucket for the bottle to be placed in and the cork (fed by a coned hopper on the top) would be driven home by the machine's action. From here the bottle would go on yet another circular rotatable table and be swung around again, to meet the person on the labelling machine. Once labelled the bottles would go on the table at the end of the process to be boxed or crated up as required. It was primitive but it worked.

Over by the wall, and no longer in use, was my old nemesis a Purdy labelling machine but it was clear that Clive Bird was trying to make changes - with a brand new high-tech labelling machine!

This, however, looked rather comical sitting between the old-fashioned machinery on either side of it and was full of 'health & safety' features such as Perspex doors that had to be opened and shut to access any blockages on the machine. Considerate though these features were they made access to vital areas more laborious. The new machine was not a howling success; glue would often get on the pads designed to flatten the label onto the bottle, and you needed a lot of patience operating it. But it was a start at trying to upgrade the plant.

Gus and Bob were my colleagues on the line. Gus originally from the Caribbean I liked a great deal, he was easy to get along with, had a good sense of humour, and was open to new ways of working and suggestions. He was an intelligent man who I felt had never been able to develop there.

Bob however was different, very much of the era; he was more set in his ways, and often used to go on about being on "piece work". He was a simpler person, a good worker, and we all got on well.

We made the best of our time working together on the line and had some fun when we could. Bob was not averse to the odd tipple, and one of the traditions of bottling of course was to sample the wares before bottling commenced. On one occasion I remember Bob sampled several glasses of the wares (egged on by some other members of staff who wandered into the bottling room) so much so that he was drunk and as he stood there with his head drooped down and talking gibberish, we wondered how we would get him out at the end of the day. None of us wanted to see him get into trouble.

As you passed through the small door within the fire shutter at the day's end you had to make sure you ducked your head. Incapable of getting through the door on his own I can remember we guided his head down low enough to clear the top of the door, so as not to be poleaxed in trying! Urging Bob to keep as quiet as possible and steadying him on either side, thankfully the Foreman had not noticed his condition. As we sent Bob off mumbling away to himself in the right direction, he seemed more than confident (and happy!) that he could make his way home!

An example of doing things a bit different is when I suggested it might be an idea to thoroughly steam clean the bottling machine. Remarkably, to my knowledge and theirs, this had never been done (within living memory) but had been standard practice at IBWS. Gus was more than keen to do something new, and Bob too liked the idea, so we stripped the machine down took it all apart and gave it a thorough steam through, which took a good few hours. Clive Bird saw what we were doing and was more than happy with it.

It has to be said that given that this was not standard practice Cullen's had got off remarkably lightly regarding problems with their bottlings, so credit to those who bottled in the past.

Clive Bird was also trying to instil something new I felt and break away from the rigid discipline of the past set-up. It was clear from the men's demeanour in general that they were not encouraged in any way to think for themselves. This is no criticism of the previous manager, who no doubt had his own reasons for handling it in such a way.

THE WINES

A number of wines of course were bottled by Cullen's then, reds, whites, and fortified and the ones I particularly remember were those of Bouchard Père & Fils, Egri Bikavér's Bulls Blood, Cyprus and South African Sherries, plus one special wine then that certainly fitted my interest!

This particular wine did not arrive at the warehouse in the usual manner by tanker but was sent direct, in wood, from Portugal from the lodges of Offley Forrester & Co Ltd. in Vila Nova de Gaia. To see the cask (known as a pipe) of port arrive was special in another way too as it was becoming increasingly rare to see wines shipped in wood to merchants in the UK then. Most bottlings now took place in

Portugal, so it was the last of a dying process which had once been common in the British wine trade, and certainly carried out regularly at Cullen's Waterloo Arches in the past.

However, things did not go smoothly. Firstly, it was how to get the pipe (of some 550 litres) up to the bottling floor. The only way seemed to be by lift, and this meant that antiquated affair that never did fill you with confidence from a safety point of view!

As the pipe was rolled, pushed and shoved into the lift on the ground floor it began to make its slow trudging journey upward, at what seemed to be about one mile an hour! Before long the lift ground to a halt between floors. It became clear that the sheer weight of the port pipe had set the lift-off balance so now it was stuck. I seem to recall someone (perhaps Clive Bird) managing to open the lift gate between the floors and try and redistribute the weight – this was not for the faint-hearted of course and dangerous, but it worked, and the lift continued painfully upward, at perhaps, still, one mile an hour!

Once eventually rolled into the bottling room and rested it was bottled directly from the cask and as far as I can recall not filtered. This would make sense as this was an aged old tawny style which would be best to bottle in its natural state. I felt a sense of pride when we bottled the wine, and it was the last time this was ever done at Cullen's.

The label for the Offley 'Four Feathers' Tawny that was bottled that day. Previous Cullen's price lists show that in the past they bottled one, two and three feathers during the height of port wine's popularity.

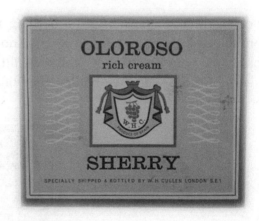

Some examples of Cullen labels of the time. They reflect the age itself where label design was fairly rudimentary. The Bouchard Père & Fils is in the classic Burgundian style and the logo and design are still used by the company today.

THE CELLARS

One area I found particularly fascinating and liked to visit was the lower cellar in the basement as here you had a true sense of the traditional wine trade. I remember one of the small brick cubby holes holding six or seven bottles of Chateau Latour 1970, all covered in dust and as I gently lifted one out to take a look one of the older warehouse staff eyed me with a distaining look as if to say you mustn't touch. This did not deter me, and I just wanted to explore further the cellars and their contents.

If there was a bottling of a particularly good claret or burgundy then these would be laid down in the traditional wrought-iron bins to mature. I can recall being taught how to lay the bottles down correctly on the 'lards' (the wooden slats that went between each layer). If you did not do this right the contents would tend to sink inwards, and eventually, the lot could come crashing down!

An example of a wrought-iron wine bin with the lards placed between each layer.

There were many interesting fine wines stored in the cellar and it was a treasure trove of small parcels and lots, some put aside many years ago, silently maturing.

Of course, it was port wine that really held a fascination for me and I recall Warre's 1963 Vintage Port, some 1970s (Croft, Sandeman and Warre's), along with the first vintage port I ever drank Cockburn's 1967. I was taken aback by the sheer elegance of this wine and understood why a vintage port was so special.

At the back of the cellar was the impressive sight of at least 60 wooden boxes of Offley Boa Vista 1972 Vintage Port. This was a lighter vintage but still had a lot of charm when I tasted it.

A case end from one of the Offley Vintage ports from the Cullen's cellar.

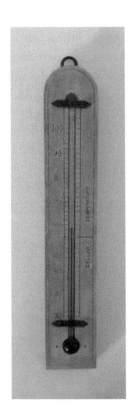

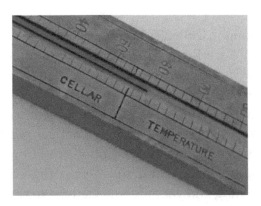

The last remnant of the Cullen's cellar in Battersea. The temperature
thermometer.

As time went on the familiarity of the routine began to grind and I felt a sense of stagnation, I knew that if I wanted to progress in wine I had to learn more. In the trade, this meant taking the Wine & Spirit Education Trust courses. I had decided that if I took the courses I would finance them myself and I did not want the company to pay, so I was accountable to myself to do as well as I could.

For a cellar staff in Cullen's doing such courses was unheard of, and I kept this low-key. One day however in the canteen I did take my wine course book in to read during the break. Sitting next to me was a young lad called Martin, who was always then brazen, slightly immature and a touch cocky who slowly lent back on the two legs of the old wooden chair so that he could glance into what I was reading. "What have you got there?" he said, to which I told him I was studying a book on wine. You could see this was a complete anathema to him and the thoughts of anything to do with studying were abhorrent.

Strangely enough, as time went by I noticed a change in his personality. What had happened in his life I do not know, but the immaturity had gone and he had become more adult in his manner.

Growing increasingly frustrated and not seeing any chance of progressing I began to think about the possibility of working elsewhere and started to look at retail opportunities.

Not unreasonably I thought Cullen's themselves may be a start, so applied for a position at the Battersea Park Road wine branch. The protocol was that this meant going for an Interview at Cullen's head office at Parsonage House in Dorking, where I was to meet with a Mr. Cullen (one of many in the family business). The interview went well enough, and as I left I suddenly realised the one thing we had not discussed was the wage itself! However, not long after my return to the warehouse in the afternoon I suddenly got a phone call from Mr. Cullen asking me whether I was available that evening to go into the shop and run it! I was astounded, I had no training and yet they expected me to run a shop! I realised then that they were not serious in their approach, and declined the job outright.

Not long after this, I remember meeting James Rogers in the warehouse and he had asked me about the shop position which I told him I had declined.

At this point in time, James was creating a name for himself within the wine trade and putting Cullen's more and more on the map with effective PR, and a new approach to wine retailing. But, curiously, it was an interview I went to with another small retailer, Daly & Mallis, which proved that not all appreciated his talents.

As far as I can recall the Daly & Mallis head office was in Burnt Oak and they had several shops around London. By comparison to Cullen's the office seemed very hi-tech, with big grey computers, open-planned and spacious with plenty of office staff.

I was then invited into Mr. Mallis's office for an interview with him. I immediately found him a confident, slightly overbearing character, who no sooner had I sat down wanted to show me the next "big thing", of which he was extremely proud – a new brand of Sangria he had invented with a 'blood red' painted bottle! To be honest I thought it looked ghastly. As the Interview progressed I soon discovered it had little to do with me, but more an opportunity to make his views plain on James Rogers. Being from Cullen's I was the ideal vessel to vent his opinion on. One claim was that James spent far too much time trying to promote Cullen's with various celebrities. I could not help noticing as he said this that several pictures on his office walls were of him with - well - celebrities, in the same fashion. One in particular I remember was him with Cilla Black. The whole interview had been a sham.

One more meaningful Interview I recall was with the buyer for the Tate Gallery restaurant, Millbank. Although I did not have the experience then for the position I was applying for he advised me to try and join a wine wholesaler, something I took on board, and appreciated his advice. The idea of working in retail eventually began to wane and I continued to work with Gus and Bob on the bottling line and in the warehouse. By this time I preferred to have my breaks and lunch in the bottling room itself, the trudge to the tea room seemed both pointless and depressing, and both Gus and Bob followed suit. I was enjoying the Wine & Spirit Education Trust courses however and particularly I recall the Higher Certificate.

This meant a journey over to Mansion House in the City, one evening a week, and

I did the best I could and achieved a 'Distinction' on the higher certificate course which I was proud of at the time. I would subsequently go on to the WSET Diploma.

One day whilst walking through the warehouse near the office Paul Tholen who was in charge of the Cullen's Wine Club stopped me to say he had heard I had done the higher certificate course and done well. I think Paul was on the WSET board and as I had not told anyone in the offices that I was taking the courses he seemed naturally surprised. I had asked my mother to keep it quiet also.

The one thing that struck me about doing the courses and the Cullen wine range was just how eclectic it was. Some of the most obscure of wines mentioned in the courses from areas in France, such as Jura with Chateau Chalon, or reds from the Loire, such as Chinon were stocked. German wines were also very popular at the time, but the range was equally forward-thinking, with a Sheurebe in litre bottles being very popular. Even Austria with its rarely seen Ausbruch was sold, something of a rarity then. The range really did seem to be like an educational resource.

AN OFFICE MOVE - A NEW HORIZON

Not long after this, I remember being called into the office by James Rogers to see whether I could work with Tommy Lambert, the buyer and Eric Pateman, his assistant in the buying office for maybe one or two days a week. The idea was, amongst other things, to take stock in the warehouse from the various suppliers and to help prepare orders.

There were no computers at that point within Cullen's so all stock levels were recorded on a box card holder system involving many cards from numerous suppliers. Each card held the name of the supplier (for example Hedges & Butler) and listed below the number of lines Cullen's purchased from them. This could mean wines, spirits, liqueurs, beers etc. which would be located at different points all around the vast warehouse.

I thoroughly enjoyed darting around the warehouse from one location to another with a pad to prepare an order, and with Eric Pateman's guidance would collate the order which would be rung through to the supplier.

I do recall that such was my memory at that time for the products in the warehouse I could pinpoint the exact location of every line, and give a fairly good estimate of its stock levels based on the product and its speed of sale, before actually going to the location itself.

The office that the three of us sat in at this time was incredibly small, with Tommy Lambert sitting at the back at the main desk, Eric to his right, and me at a desk near the doorway. James Rogers, Paul Tholen and the office girls were located further down the building. The office was so small you could hardly move, and in time a more spacious office area would be built for all concerned on the Battersea Park Road side of the building, but for now, this was it.

It was here that Tommy Lambert would receive visits from the various reps or suppliers. He was also coming toward the end of his tenure as the Buyer and Eric Pateman would take over from him. Tommy was always friendly, helpful and encouraging. His personal life, caring for his wife who was unwell, meant that he was rarely able to get a full night's sleep, and at times (after a couple of lunchtime drinks) would be seen to nod off in the afternoons in his office chair. I remember on one occasion James Rogers seeing this and this perhaps reflected James's character, he simply gently pulled the door closed to allow Tommy to sleep on.

I thoroughly enjoyed the two days in the office and would return to the warehouse for the remainder of the week. Certain jobs however required more than two days.

One aspect of the wine trade then which used to cause a great deal of commotion was the coming of the Budget. For retailers, it was an opportunity to cajole the consumer into the fear of a duty increase, be it on wine spirits or beer, and a rush would ensue before the prices would go up. Buying at 'pre-budget prices' was a trade favourite, but sales did increase considerably and the shops would take in extra stocks in anticipation of this demand.

One job post-budget was to produce a new price list for the shops, and I remember my ability to write incredibly small seemed to come into demand as alterations (both to listings and pricing) had to be made to the list to reflect the increases.

It was whilst I was doing this one day that Nigel Blundell of Walter Siegel & Co Ltd came to see James Rogers and Eric Pateman. He was friendly and amusing and commented on me working on the list and I think was impressed by the tiny script!

It was also in this cramped office one day that I saw James give a very convincing argument to a gentleman from IDV (International Distillers and Vintners) on why Cullen's should NOT stock their popular brand Piat'd'Or. They had obviously drafted in their top man for this meeting, but James took a very dim view of branded wines and really it was going very much against his ethos of discovering wines purely on the merit of their quality and price. I remember listening very intently to James's viewpoint and being impressed.

However, unknown to the gentleman from IDV the meeting had come about as several shops had asked if they could stock the wine. It was heavily advertised at the time, both on television and on hoardings and a popular brand.

The conclusion of the meeting was that it would not be stocked and the gentleman from IDV having put up a valiant fight was clear on James's view. The meeting had been a long one, and rather wearily the gentleman left the office down the stairs on his way out to the loading bay. It was whilst he was on his way out that James then suddenly said to me to go and catch him up and ask him to come back. Once he was back in the office James then said he would allow shops to stock the product but only on a direct delivery basis, much to the relief of the gentleman from IDV.

There was probably more at play here than simply stocking that brand as will be explained later, but it was also James's way of placating his shop managers. As it turned out James was correct, the brand would eventually fade away to be replaced by the next big thing, and so on.

JAMES ROGERS

The building of more spacious offices, a larger area for the office girls and manager, and for the buying office, plus separate offices for James Rogers and Paul Tholen, was very welcome by all.

It was also around this time that things began to change for my mother too. She and James had always got on well, and my mother was very well organised. She was now given the position as James's PA, and given how busy he was she had a job on her hands!

I was also now spending even more time in the buying office and much less in the warehouse, and hopefully proving my worth. It seemed strange to see my former colleagues Gus and Bob in the warehouse and not be part of their world in the same way as before, but I always enjoyed the times we could still work together, but it was becoming less and less.

I do remember being invited into the tasting room for the first time by James to take part. I had set things up but now was my opportunity to be involved. I was naturally nervous but would listen intently to all the comments being made. There were quite a lot of wines to taste, perhaps thirty or so, and I worked my way through them diligently. James and Paul's techniques were fascinating to watch, but more on that later.

The one thing that no one had made plain to me is that you needed to spit the wine out. Whether this was because I was so fascinated by the occasion itself, or felt a sense of embarrassment up against such seasoned users of the spittoon I can't recall, but I just drank all the samples!

Once the tasting was over my head was spinning, and with a happy smile I made my way back into the bottling room with Gus and Bob and once more on to the corking machine, which I stared at with an inebriated grin, and the monotonous repetition of driving the corks home into the bottle seemed less tedious! As far as I can recall this was one of the last times I worked with Gus and Bob and from here on it was in the buying office.

What also seemed strange now was that I was working in the more spacious office with Eric Pateman, now the Buyer (after Tommy Lambert's retirement), and to the left of where I sat my mother too! It was always fascinating to watch the interaction between James and my mother first thing in the morning when he arrived.

My mother had to the left of where she sat a small table which had the all-important rich tea biscuits on it plus the electric kettle and cups. James would present himself to attention in front of my mother in his double-breasted suit, always with a smile and a pleasant greeting (him calling her Pat and her James). He would then ask her who had been in contact and the itinerary for the day ahead and was given the more important post. After this, he would then move next door into his office and my mother would follow a few minutes later after he settled in - with the biscuits and a much-appreciated cup of tea. To all others in the offices and warehouse, he would be referred to as Mr. James, only Paul Tholen and the senior managers simply calling him James.

James was always the hive of productivity, and from my mother's viewpoint, that meant his regular use of the Dictaphone. He would often sit at his desk taping his conversations which my mother would then type up for him, be it simple correspondence, to long works or articles for magazines. He was prolific and demanding, and would then go through the typed results with her and make the necessary adjustments. He would also ask her for her opinion and thoughts.

For my mother of course who did not have a wine background, James would present her with one or two words that she felt she needed to keep close at hand as a spelling reference, as they were constantly being used. I still have her small Collins Gem dictionary.

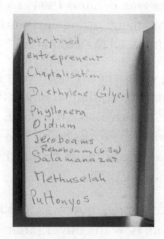

It is interesting to note in her dictionary Diethylene Glycol. This would have referred to the Austrian wine scandal of 1985. Cullen's also stocked a range of Austrian wines at the time.

I found it fascinating to work with James, he had immense drive, and conviction in his beliefs, and what seemed like a radically different approach to wine. He was an inspiration to work with and his enthusiasm was infectious. He was highly intelligent but always approachable, and inventive. He introduced the Cullen Wine Club, the wine warehouse concept, and new ways of regenerating the W. H. Cullen wine chain through the introduction of the more modern sounding 'Cullens' (dropping the W. H.) Gourmet & Goblet and Winemart shops (all geared to particular socio-economic areas). I also liked the fact that if he was wrong about anything he would freely admit it, and take responsibility for his actions.

He was of course also running the wine division of Cullen's (at this point some 90 shops) so it was interesting to see his management style. Very rarely did he ever lose his temper, and he delegated well, expecting others to perform and would not interfere unless required to do so.

Passing his office on one occasion I remember him making a phone call to Oz Clarke, and on reaching his answerphone message, James chuckling away at Oz Clarke's message!

He was also clever at promoting Cullen's within what would be called today the celebrity circuit. I remember several actors coming into the tasting room Terence Alexander being one, who was convivial, and also Auberon Waugh the journalist when we were still operating from the small buying office. Above my desk by the door in the office was a large map of France pinpointing of course all the vineyards etc. He stared at this almost motionless for a good ten minutes and chose not to converse with anyone in the office, waiting purely to be ushered in by James to the tasting room.

Another frequent visitor was Simon Loftus from the Adnams Brewery in Suffolk, who was very keen on wine, and you could see him enjoy his conversations with James in the tasting room.

TASTING TECHNIQUE

Friday afternoons were the highlight of the week. I would be asked to prepare the room for a tasting, which I thoroughly enjoyed. Originally foil had been used to cover the bottles from being identified, but as luck would have it a supplier had given us a collection of cardboard packing hoods which slipped ideally over the bottles.

What was fascinating to watch was James' technique. With both him Paul Tholen, and Eric Pateman in the room there wasn't a lot of space, the room was thin and narrow, but it was a hive of activity!

James would move up the line extremely fast checking the wine's aroma first, and then head back taking small sips. From here on he would rush to and fro, and taste very quickly. He would dart back and forth and narrow down the wines which really impressed him, pulling them forward for re-tasting. From here he would often make a guess as to where the wine was from - and was invariably right.

Within this may be some wines from the existing Cullen's range as a comparison, but invariably they were new samples from suppliers.

Paul Tholen would be equally as busy as James and all present were to give their opinions on the wines. He would listen carefully to everyone's comments and was never dictatorial, or try and sway others. Despite all this experience around me I put my views forward too and learnt quickly.

There was no way a spittoon could operate in such a small environment, so the poor sink came in for some rough treatment as they jockeyed for position. I remember Paul Tholen had a very impressive distance and power on his delivery!

James was often so busy he would often be called to deal with one question or another from the other staff so was constantly moving in and out of the tasting room, but still somehow managed to hold his concentration.

I remember on one particular Friday James asked me to prepare a purely Cabernet Sauvignon tasting. In the room were Cabernet's from nearly every corner of the wine globe, including an example from Spain which was unusual then. It must have been at least twenty wines. I arranged them how I thought best based on geography and characteristics and covered them with the hoods as usual.

In what was a quieter afternoon than many James began to work his way through them in his usual fashion. I stood by the doorway and watched him operate throughout. By the end of the tasting, he then decided to tell me where the wines were from, and to my amazement, he identified all the countries correctly! I was so taken aback by this; that I suddenly said spontaneously "That was very good!" He turned around smiling and simply said "thank you". Here I was telling the MD what a fine job he had done!

I set up and took part in many more tastings over this period, and learnt a great deal from James and Paul Tholen, by watching and observing.

A TASTE OF THINGS TO COME

It is very interesting to look back at a Cullen list from 1979 and see the gradual changes taking place. The New World in the form of California is very much in its embryonic stage and both Argentina and Chile are featured for the first time. James has written the comments here and suggested for the first time that the New World may challenge the Old.

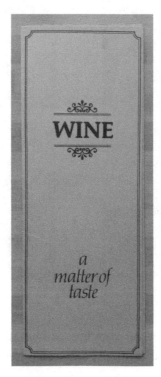

By experimenting and being a little more adventurous we have found some exceptionally fine wines which can proudly stand alongside the best that France and Germany can offer. This selected list combines the old world with the new, the traditional with the less conventional, and all are excellent value for money.

These will bring enjoyment to those who regard wine as a pleasurable pastime or hobby rather than a hospitable necessity. We would very much appreciate any comments you would like to make on any of them.

Subject to stock availability, all these wines can be ordered through our branches. You are welcome, if you prefer, to ring 01-622-4467 and ask for wines to be delivered to your local branch.

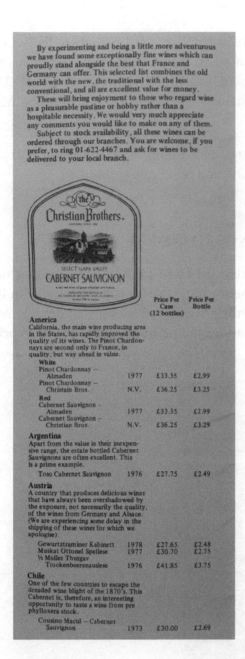

America
California, the main wine producing area in the States, has rapidly improved the quality of its wines. The Pinot Chardonnays are second only to France, in quality, but way ahead in value.

		Price Per Case (12 bottles)	Price Per Bottle
White			
Pinot Chardonnay – Almaden	1977	£33.35	£2.99
Pinot Chardonnay – Christain Bros.	N.V.	£36.25	£3.25
Red			
Cabernet Sauvignon – Almaden	1977	£33.35	£2.99
Cabernet Sauvignon – Christian Bros.	N.V.	£36.25	£3.29

Argentina
Apart from the value in their inexpensive range, the estate bottled Cabernet Sauvignons are often excellent. This is a prime example.

Toso Cabernet Sauvignon	1976	£27.75	£2.49

Austria
A country that produces delicious wines that have always been overshadowed by the exposure, not necessarily the quality, of the wines from Germany and Alsace. (We are experiencing some delay in the shipping of these wines for which we apologise).

Gewurtztraminer Kabinett	1978	£27.65	£2.48
Muskat Ottonel Spatlese	1977	£30.70	£2.75
½ Muller Thurgav Trockenbeerenauslese	1976	£41.85	£3.75

Chile
One of the few countries to escape the dreaded wine blight of the 1870's. This Cabernet is, therefore, an interesting opportunity to taste a wine from pre phylloxera stock.

Cousino Macul – Cabernet Sauvignon	1973	£30.00	£2.69

Germany
For your interest, we have selected just two superb wines from the Rhine and Mosel:

		Price Per Case (12 bottles)	Price Per Bottle
Rhine			
Deidesheimer Herrgottsacker Riesling Kabinett QMP	1977	£36.30	£3.25
Mosel			
Trittenheimer Apotheke Riesling Kabinett QMP	1977	£43.00	£3.85

Greece
It's not all Retsina and Ouzo! Frankly, this is the first Greek wine I have ever really enjoyed. One of the reasons is due to its maturation in French Oak Casks.

Nemea	1975	£22.20	£1.99

Hungary
This 5 Puttonos (Class 1) luscious Tokay is a unique dessert wine (ideal to drink with the Christmas pudding!)

Tokay d'Aszu	1973	£31.10	£2.79

Italy
We have included two 'Classicos' and two of the fine wines from Piemonte. Only the Barolo, although drinking well now, can be laid down.

Red			
Valpolicella Classico - Sartori	1974	£22.20	£1.99
Chianti Classico	1976	£22.20	£1.99
Barbaresco	1975	£28.90	£2.59
Barolo	1974	£37.35	£3.35
White			

Although reds from Italy generally outclass their white counterparts, this Verdicchio must be included.

Verdicchio	1977	£24.00	£2.15

South Africa
South Africa is better known for its Sherries than its table wines. However, the latter are excellent quality and represent great value.

Red			
Roodeberg	1974	£24.40	£2.19
Cabernet Sauvignon	1975	£26.65	£2.39
White			
Chenin Blanc	1978	£22.20	£1.99

Portugal
We have just added this mature Dao to our list. As full and smooth as the fine wines from the Rhone.

Dao Garrafeira	1970	£29.60	£2.65

Spain
A country whose reputation has suffered greatly from the amount of inferior wine that can be purchased. But, both Penedes and Rioja produce superb quality wines.

Penedes - The House of Torres			
Vina Sol (white)	1977	£23.65	£2.12
Coronas	1976	£26.80	£2.40
Vina Esmeralda (white)	1978	£32.70	£2.93
Rioja - White Burgundy devotees will enjoy the Metropol.			
Metropol (white)	1973	£26.65	£2.39
Vina Zaco	1969	£27.35	£2.45
Vina Ardanza	1973	£33.35	£2.99
Reserva 904	1964	£43.40	£3.89

There is no mention here yet on the list of the first of James's famous 'finds' Chateau Musar, from the most unlikely of places, Lebanon. I remember trying this serious, deep-flavoured wine for the first time and being impressed by its forest berry fruit and depth of flavour.

MR. TODOROV

If there was one country that has been associated with James more than any other it is Bulgaria. But in reality, he brought wines from so many other areas of the wine world to the public's attention that this is often forgotten, as can be seen in the list.

Not that all these New World wine regions were successful, that was impossible to achieve, but what he did make people see was the world of wine was not simply the staples of the old world, France, Italy, Spain and Germany. Within these particular countries, changes were also taking place and new ground was being broken, with winemakers making more modern styles, and promoting grape varieties. All inspired by New World thinking.

When I joined the wine trade in the early years the offerings from areas such as France or Spain at the lower end were pretty dire, but as there was no other choice, the public just went with it. The producers were selling wines which were often poor and reaping a good reward, and it is not hard to see how a branded wine offered what at least appeared to be a wine of more reasonable quality, and consistency. James wanted to show that with a bit of education and imagination the public could do better than this.

In 1980 James introduced a wine country which really was about to change the whole balance of the trade and expectations of the drinking public – Australia. Nigel Blundell of Walter Siegel & Co Ltd recalls his memories of that time in section 28.

But the arrival of Mr. Todorov at the offices from the Bulgarian Vintner Company was something I always recall. As in the 1980s shoulder pads were the *de rigueur* for ladies, so Mr. Todorov harked back to the 1960s with an impressive jacket which Leonid Brezhnev would have fought over for shoulder pads alone! In fact his jacket seemed more like armour, which looked as if it was reinforced with bent rounded plywood around his sizable frame, with no suggestion of a crease anywhere, and the material just stuck onto it!

Mr. Todorov would often leave with considerable orders from Cullen's; with two full containers on order at any one time, plus more following on quickly thereafter. He sported a ready smile when leaving; a firm handshake stretching from his tubular reinforced sleeve, and a look that said that anything and everything was possible!

Whilst these shipments would contain whites (which were not particularly good or representative of the given grape variety) the reds were, given the price, impressive, with the Cabernet Sauvignon from Svishtov being extremely popular. Indigenous varieties such as Mavrud and Gamza made up small quantities within the container loads as their more rustic styles were less commercially appealing.

I do remember one thing that amazed us just how long a particular vintage seemed to last. I do recall having a conversation with James and that the Svishtov Cabernet Sauvignon 1981 seemed to be going on for some considerable time?! By way of luck, squirrelled away in the tasting room, was a bottle from one of the very early shipments. He asked me to go into the warehouse and pick a bottle from the most recent arrival, and on a tasting comparison, they were like chalk and cheese! The wine was still good, but clearly, the vintage had been stretched to an impossible degree.

WINE WARS

Less desirable attention came Cullen's way in 1982 with an event that at the time caused quite a bit of consternation – the Falklands War.

It was interesting in a way as this was probably the first time since the end of World War Two, with attitudes towards German wines that jingoism would come into play.

Cullen's had been selling very successfully up until this point an Argentinian wine, rather cheekily named Franchette. With its French-sounding overtones few customers probably even registered its origins, but now given the crisis it was taking centre stage at head office.

I remember the red was a full-bodied and powerful wine, and typical of wines at that time from South America, the white was less impressive but still very drinkable. The wines arrived in bulk tankers at Battersea and I can recall being on the bottling line and bottling large quantities of the red.

Now that the Falklands crisis occurred there was suddenly a dilemma, and with passions running high in the press any connection with a product of Argentinian origin was bound to cause suggestions of unpatriotic behaviour, which they would pounce on!

For James, it was a problem, and he asked the opinion of all those around him and then made his decision.

In the end, as far as I can recall, James relied on the good common sense of the English drinking public. There was little to be gained in destroying the wine, it had after all been paid for and arrived before all this had even begun.

He would leave it to the buying public to pass the final verdict. If there were those who felt strongly enough about it and didn't want to purchase it so be it and those who wished to could. I remember a circular was produced for the shops to explain this viewpoint, and in the end, the wine sold out. The customers had passed their verdict.

COMPUTERISATION

As with so many other businesses in the 1980s computerisation loomed, and the decision to enter what seemed like a shaky new technology then, fraught with uncertainties as to the reliability of both programmes and hardware, did little to fill those who would use it with confidence.

Cullen's stepped into the fray a little later than some, but it was clear, we were told, that this was the future.

It was decided that for the office staff a familiarisation course was needed and the larger office was decked out with tables and chairs in a U shape, whilst at the other end there was a large lone grey IBM computer and keyboard with a gentleman sitting by it. Everyone sat around looking rather embarrassed at sitting opposite each other as the lessons began.

The tutor himself was a German gentleman who explained what the technology was about, who I seem to recall whose English was not particularly clear. It was either this (or possibly combined) that most of the staff present was so flummoxed by this new technology that they simply didn't understand.

I don't think anybody actually had a go on the computer itself we simply looked at it and passed by rather like a slow funeral cortege! All we did know was that this gentleman was being paid a staggering £25 an hour for his services! (A huge amount of money then), and all came away bewildered and less than confident.

For those who were to use this technology in the ordering system for the shops, it would be a difficult time. The office manager in charge then was Alan Fiddament. Alan was a very amiable man who was popular with the girls in the office and was good friends with Eric Pateman and Clive Bird.

But, the transition to this new technology strained relationships to the core. I recall being in the buying office one day when Alan burst in furious with Eric Pateman over some problem that had occurred connected with the computer system. Eric was calm by nature and listened to the outburst without commenting, which was so out of character from Mr. Fiddament, but the pressure had become just too much.

The next day I recall Alan came into the office and went up to Eric's desk and in front of us all apologised to Eric for the outburst the previous day. I remember being so impressed by his actions they really did exemplify his true character.

The computerisation of the shop ordering system did not extend to the buying office which was still done on the box card system.

NOVEAU OLD AND NEW AND INNOVATIONS

Cullen's also at this time, like so many other retailers, was often in the grip of Beaujolais Nouveau fever when the release came around in November. Today it is hard to relay just how popular Beaujolais Nouveau was then, and much was made of getting the first shipments over and hurrying the wine into the shops. Huge volumes were sold.

As a twist on this James came up with the idea of doing something a little different. Being that the harvest in the southern hemisphere fell between February and April he promoted the theme of a southern hemisphere 'Nouveau' with white wines from New Zealand amongst them.

As more and more countries from around the wine globe were added he also purchased several shop window automata. In their striking national costumes, these moving mannequins were an original centrepiece of many a Cullen's shop window display.

Amongst the other small jobs I recall, was giving James the heads up when a vintage wine was getting low in the cellars, so he could put some cases aside before it ran out. This would range from chateau wines to vintage ports and I recall Ch. Pichon Longueville Baron and Branaire Ducru 1975 in their wooden cases being amongst them, plus some Warre's 1963 and several other fine wines. It was normally around two cases of each chateau wine, which were put into one of the many little alcoves in the low ceilinged cellar and stowed away for him.

CHRISTMAS 1984

As with all wine retailers, the run-up to Christmas is the tense key point in the calendar in getting things right! The shop managers were naturally vocal if they were not happy with a lack of stock availability and James was well aware of this. In the buying office with Eric Pateman, I was extremely busy rushing around trying to ensure all the lines were covered and orders placed in good time for the shops to draw from the warehouse. The box card system went into overdrive!

For James himself I recall him saying to me one day that this was the time of year he liked least as a decision had to be made as to which supplier he backed to promote for the Christmas season. Offers from these large concerns, such as Matthew Clark, Hedges and Butler, Seagrams plus others, would all be put forward for consideration and would cover a multitude of lines. He knew he could only back one, and the others would be disappointed their bid was rejected. This probably explains the earlier encounter with the gentleman from IDV and Piat'd'Or, there was much more at stake.

As we moved beyond Christmas and into the New Year I remember James calling Eric and I into his office. He congratulated us both that for the first time he had not received any complaints about stock levels from the shops. We had got it right, and I remember feeling proud of that achievement at the time and receiving due recognition. All the hard work had paid off.

THE SMITH WOODHOUSE AWARD

Moving into 1985 this would be a memorable year in more ways than one, a fast-paced year with many changes afoot.

On the plus side an advert that appeared in Harpers Wine & Spirit Gazette on the 1st February caught my eye, the Smith Woodhouse Port Wine Award.

My interest in port had been ongoing for several years, in fact, one of the first books I ever received on port wine was from my mother in 1982, Wyndham Fletcher's 'Port – An Introduction to its History and Delights' which she has written an inscription in. The chapter on the reminiscence of his life in the port wine trade in the 1930s, and thereafter, at the back of the book has always fascinated me.

Here was an opportunity it seemed to put what knowledge I had on the subject to the test at least, and the competition was designed for 'young members of the wine trade' as was stated, which, at that point in time, I was. The details of the requirements can be seen on the page itself.

I beavered away on the project studiously and did my level best to make a reasonable presentation. Eventually, it was finished and I submitted my efforts. I had not mentioned it to anyone at Cullen's that I had entered the competition, preferring to just wait and see the outcome. But, more on this later, further changes were now about to take place.

THE
SMITH WOODHOUSE
AWARD

As part of the double centenary of Smith Woodhouse (founded 1784) an annual award is announced, sponsored jointly by Smith Woodhouse and UK agents John E Fells & Sons. The award will be called The Smith Woodhouse Award.

The Award:
The winning candidate will be invited, all expenses paid, to be the guest of Smith Woodhouse during the vintage period for three days. The winner will be tutored in all aspects of blending, tasting and maturing of port, together with visits to lodges and to Douro quintas. (At the discretion of the examiners, two awards may from time to time be given).

Requirements:
A pass in the Wine & Spirit Education Trust Higher Certificate; aged between 20 and 30 years on 1 January of the year of each award; two years minimum wine trade experience, or in hotel catering.

Projects:
1 To submit an essay of between 1000 and 1500 words, on: Are there too many styles of port? Discuss.
2 In addition, the candidate's views on marketing port in Great Britain are required in a separate paper, its length at the discretion of the writer.

Entries:
To be submitted by 30th April 1985 to John E Fells & Sons, Fells House, Birkbeck Grove, London W3 7QD. Essays should be written, neatly, on A4 paper. The envelope containing the work should be marked 'Scholarship' on the top left hand corner.

Examining Board:
Two Directors of Smith Woodhouse; Miss Serena Sutcliffe M W; I Emeny, Managing Director of John E Fells & Sons; W A Warre M W, Director of John E Fells & Sons.

Fells
Founded in 1858
at Love Lane in the City of London

John E Fells & Sons Ltd, Fells House, Birkbeck Grove, London W3 7QD
Telephone: 01-749 3661

THE TAKEOVER

Around March of 1985 some very disturbing news came through, that Cullen's was the subject of a takeover bid.

We of course knew little of what was occurring but it was an extremely tense time. The head office at Cullen's in Battersea had always had a family feel about it, and the thoughts that this may change were hard to contemplate, so we all waited anxiously to hear the latest news on developments.

The takeover bid that took place then has been described elsewhere as 'aggressive' and this may well have been the case. What was clear at the time was that Cullen's grocery side of the business was finding competition from the supermarkets tough. The delicatessen approach for which Cullen's was famous then was falling out of fashion, and their image as a purely upmarket grocery retailer meant that it had a limited appeal to only those who could afford to shop there. The supermarkets were beginning to offer these specialities, and much more besides, and tightened their grip.

I recall Cullen's grocery side was becoming increasingly involved with Nisa for the first time in an attempt to enter the more commercial mainstream market.

The bid now led to tensions between the two families, the Cullen's on the grocery side of the business and the Rogers on the wine side. James's father had run the wine division in the past and I remember one of the Cullen lorry drivers had been a batman to Mr. Rogers senior when he served in the army in World War Two. James was the great-grandson of John Cullen.

Whilst David Cullen and the other directors in Dorking wanted to take the company in one direction, namely keeping the grocery side going, James wanted to keep the wine side alive. He had worked hard to promote Cullen's as a new innovative wine merchant, and it was recognised as such. We simply had to wait on the side-lines for the outcome as the battle to win control continued over the proceeding months.

I remember on one occasion whilst in the buying office during this period seeing James come in one morning looking totally and utterly exhausted. I had never seen him like this before, gaunt, dark under the eyes, shattered. He had been driving all night traversing the country in an attempt to get the backing of as many of the small Cullen shareholders as he could to back his cause.

Eventually, after this unhappy family feud the outcome became clear, James had won. Promises were made to keep the wine division going and we all expressed a sigh of relief, but who exactly had bought the company?

One morning James came into the buying office smiling to introduce the new owners to us, who we simply knew as 'three ex-Imperial group employees'. I took one look at the three gentlemen with their fixed stern expressions and remarked to my mother that I didn't think they were for real. As it turned out, I was right.

It soon became clear that their real intention was to asset strip the company, the top twelve wine shops would eventually go on to be sold to Threshers, but in the meantime, the company and the head office in Battersea would be wound down. The Cullen name and some shops would of course exist but in a very small way. It must have been a devastating blow to James.

BUYING TIME AND AN APPRECIATION

The news, it is true to say, really focused our minds, and for many who worked for Cullen's had massive implications. Many of the staff, including Clive Bird lived in rented accommodation above a Cullen shop, so not only was there the worry of losing their job but also where they lived.

I think James was attempting to keep things running for as long as he possibly could before the closure, to buy time and also plan his next move.

Before the final closure, he wanted to show his appreciation to all the Cullen wine shop managers for their dedication by taking them on a day trip to France! I remember thinking how on earth would he achieve this as it meant taking all the ninety-plus managers out of their shops for a day, but this is what he did. As far as I recall there were no assistant managers so it would simply mean the shops would shut!

The trip on the cross-channel ferry was a welcome relief from the stresses we were under at the time and I remember being at a table having a meal with others from the head office. James had also invited past employees on the trip such as Tommy Lambert and George Creffield. It was the first time I had met George Creffield who had run the Battersea warehouse before Clive Bird and had a reputation as a disciplinarian. I remember thinking how he must have mellowed in retirement as there were no signs of this in his temperament he was very genial.

The day had been a great success, but on the way back one manager had allowed his level of wine consumption to get the better of him, and James had the unfortunate task of keeping him upright and getting him past the authorities and back on board for the journey home.

FUTURE PLANS - AND DOODLINGS

Whilst this run-down period continued I remember noticing one day that James was doodling away in his office, simple pencil drawings and scribbling pictures, and variations on his initials 'JR'. He clearly had some ideas in his head but nobody knew what.

On another occasion I remember he showed us a caricature of his face holding a wine glass, but again little more was said, and nothing elaborated on.

One day completely unexpectedly James called me into his office. I was unsure what he was going to ask me but he said he had some news for me. He asked me if I would like to apply for a position with André Simon Wines who were looking for someone to do the buying at their office in Davies Street.

The idea was that he would work with me as the wine consultant for the company and I would do the day-to-day buying and liaise with him. I was taken aback by the offer and obviously very pleased. I got on well with James and had enjoyed working with him and was pleased that he felt I had the ability. He asked me not to say anything to anyone else for the time being.

Firstly I would have to have an interview with Ray Gough the owner of André Simon Wines which took place in his flat above the shop in Elizabeth Street. I was nervous but this went well enough and I was offered the position.

So James's future plan was finally out, to be a wine consultant, and this would also involve my mother. He planned to have an office in Lambeth and wanted her to come along and work there with him. I was very happy to hear this as I was concerned about what the future would bring for my mother too.

He must have reflected on this role for her as on another occasion he asked me into his office and asked me if he felt my mother would be happy working in this new environment. It would be very different for her, with less contact than at Cullen's and perhaps more isolated, but I assured him that as far as I could foresee she would be. He was concerned for her happiness too.

James's decision to become a wine consultant made sense in many ways; there were those in the trade who admired what he had achieved for Cullen's, and his reputation for a fine palate was well known. There were many other retailers and wholesalers who appreciated his talents and would like to benefit from his skills. Not just this but James also had the ability to notice talent, if he saw an individual who had passion drive and intelligence, he would recommend them to others he knew within the trade. Several in the wine trade owe part of their career progression to James. I remember being told that the financial backing for James's new venture came from one of his aunts.

All of this was to remain quiet for the moment. These were difficult times for the remainder of the Cullen staff who were all looking for new positions. Everything felt very insecure.

One other job I was asked to do via Eric Pateman from the head office in Dorking was to carry out an itinerary of the equipment we had at Battersea in the bottling room to work out its depreciation value, this was all part of the wind-down to closure. Some of the equipment was so old it had very little value, bar, of course, the relatively new idiosyncratic labelling machine!

ON THE EDGE OF MY SEAT!

In the buying office Eric Pateman still received visits from representatives, but sadly now had to inform them of the news that the company would be closing.

I remember one particular visit, that given my keen interest in port wine, I found it particularly difficult to just sit there and listen in. I felt more like I wanted to pop out of my chair!

I sat to Eric's left in the office and perhaps no more than ten feet away, but on this particular day, he had a visit from Johnny and William Graham. They had started a new port company in 1981 called Churchill Graham, and had come to see if Cullen's would be interested in stocking their wines. I sat there with a thousand questions buzzing around in my brain which I would have loved to ask them, but, painfully, I just sat there and listened in!

I remember thinking if only I could somehow get into the conversation, but the convention was that I was the assistant so, therefore, could not be involved, unless invited to. I watched intently the interaction between all three back and forth with my eyes, hoping there was an opportunity I could be brought into the conversation, but it never happened. I simply had to watch the proceedings restlessly twitching anxiously to be involved. Those questions I desperately wanted to ask would simply have to wait, for perhaps another time, if, the opportunity ever presented itself.

LOWS AND HIGHS

In the middle of June 1985, a letter dropped through the letterbox at home from John Fells & Sons Ltd. which I see now I opened in a rather hasty manner! But, to my amazement it was good news, I along with one other had 'been judged worthy of a prize', and had won the Smith Woodhouse Award. The letter was signed by W A Warre (Bill Warre).

It took some time to sink in but I was naturally delighted, and I remember telling James the news at work and him being impressed. He then asked if he could have a copy to read which he took away into his office. He was not aware I had entered the competition and later asked if he could have a further copy to give to Ray Gough.

This then really was turning into a year of lows and highs and all the more confusing for that. But never far from anyone's mind was that Cullen's was closing and that for many finding work would be extremely difficult, especially the warehouse staff, some of who had been there for many years.

James was acutely aware of this too and must have felt a huge sense of responsibility, as just before the final closure he had placed an advert in the local paper advertising experienced warehouse staff available, to do what little he could to help.

The old Cullen wine label book.

Some of the labels dated back to the early 1930s, and then moved on to the Tommy Lambert period. The book was sadly cannibalised in the 1970s and labels were removed for use in an anniversary book to mark the company's 100th year. Many pages do remain intact however and give a fascinating insight.

The old-world charm of the wine trade can be seen here in examples from the label book.

A FINAL GESTURE

In July, by way of a thank you to all the office staff at Battersea, James had arranged a farewell meal at the Institute of Directors in Pall Mall. He had held some very successful Cullen's wine tastings from here in the past for the wine club so obviously liked the location.

Both husband and wives were invited along and everyone was acutely aware this would be the final get-together before the closure. It was a sad moment naturally, but everyone put on a brave face.

The meal at the Institute of Directors top with Eric Pateman second left and George Mountford an area manager at the back. On the right is Clive Bird with Alan Fiddament third along. Below Robert Walker and me at the dinner, Robert had been instrumental in several Cullen projects, such as the wine warehouse concept. He would go on to run a Chilean wine agency.

**A final toast! James is at the back (centre) with my mother sitting next to him.
Next to her is Tommy Lambert the previous Cullen wine buyer.**

ANDRÉ SIMON WINES

The location of the André Simon's offices was in Davies Street, Mayfair and I remember arriving for the first day and going through the shop with the offices at the back, and Mr. Gough sitting at his desk.

The buying office as such was a small room downstairs in the basement which you reached by a natty 1960/70s style red spiral staircase. There were two desks one at the back on the left where a young lady called Sue Longman sat, and my intended desk which faced the stairs and had a seat in front for visitors/representatives etc. At the back was an oval sink with a work surface for placing wines for tasting. With a few grey filing cabinets thereabouts and a computer, it was all fairly compact.

The heating I seem to recollect was a Calor gas heater that gave off heady noxious fumes during the winter.

Directly opposite was a window which served no light as it was in the basement and surrounded by the three further high walls of the buildings around it. To the right of the room as you sat at the desk was a doorway that took you into the cellar area of the shop.

I remember on the first day Mr. Gough coming down to speak to me and tell me the importance of my position, and not to be taken in by certain offers by companies or swayed by their advances, something of this ilk. It was in effect a pep talk, but I was of course more than aware of this.

Mr. Gough had owned Gough Brothers, one of the large off-licence chains which he had sold to Scottish & Newcastle Brewery. He had purchased André Simon Wines which had four retail outlets all in the rather more select areas of London.

I had not yet met the person I was going to be taking over from but I think not long after Jane Hunt arrived. She was very welcoming, friendly, and put me at ease, and explained much about the company and how things worked. I always remember her saying she would generally get much more favourable buying terms on lines than I would as the men rather like to flatter in front of women, no doubt she was right!

I remember James' first arrival at André Simon perhaps a day later. He had known Ray Gough for many years (calling him Ray, and him James accordingly, but I think everyone else referred to him as Mr. Gough). He obviously wanted to bring James in as a consultant to make some changes to the retail side, and bring in some innovations and a new approach perhaps. This would be James's first consultancy job.

I recall one of the first things James did was to take a selection of French red wines, perhaps six or so from the shop to evaluate them. Just as he was going through them Jane Hunt arrived, I believe she had been at a tasting related to her MW course, and this was their first meeting.

I think she was a bit concerned about what he might think of the quality of what she had been buying but he was impressed, in fact, Jane had introduced him to one wine he was particularly impressed by and never come across, La Vieille Ferme Rouge, which has since gone on to be a major brand on the UK market.

One of the first things Jane arranged of course was for the two of us to visit the shops themselves and meet the other three managers. Jane was clearly popular with them and no doubt they were sad to see her move on. I remember the visit to Elizabeth Street and meeting the manager there. As we were talking I noticed he had a strange affliction with involuntary mouth movements in a puckering manner. I felt sorry for him but of course, I did not comment.

The other two managers we had met on the trip were friendly enough and I had met Howard at Davies Street already.

I would work with James and we would consult on new lines, offers, the wine list, visits from particular representatives, and so forth. He would make regular visits to the shop and I would also go over to his new office in Lambeth if we needed to discuss things further. This arrangement worked very well and my job title was buyer designate. We would also of course attend several wine tastings, it was a busy calendar!

The one thing that did occur to me was that whilst it may well have been Mr. Gough's wishes to introduce innovations such as the New World to the shops this would need the support of the managers themselves. This was not Cullen's where James could simply introduce what he felt was good for the company and its customers; he would need to win their support. I had also become aware of another problem that one of the managers had expected to take over from Jane when she left, and of course, that had not happened, which put me in a slightly difficult position.

I was surprised to see Mr. Gough take such little interest in the buying side, and cannot recall him ever being involved in a tasting. He seemed rather distant and aloof, happier to sit on the sideline and engage with others when he wished to.

However, one particular pleasing phone call I did receive during this period was from Bill Warre. He wanted to meet at the Ebury Wine Bar to celebrate the Smith Woodhouse Award win with a bottle of champagne before our trip to Portugal in October. For me, this was a dream come true, and at last, a chance for me to fire off all those questions! Bill was very accommodating and friendly and I enjoyed the evening a great deal. I was very appreciative, and of course, his level of knowledge was outstanding.

In the meantime, Jane continued to show me the ropes before her departure as I settled into the new role. The all-important confidential costs and terms we had with the various suppliers were once again kept in a box card system, and I was grateful for Jane's help.

THE TRIP TO PORTUGAL

On the 2nd of October I, Michael Chewter (the other winner who worked for Chaplin of Worthing at the time), and Bill Warre flew to Porto. The visit was to be over three days and it would turn out to be a fascinating experience. Paul Symington, along with Bill Warre would be our guides, and far as I can recall the itinerary for each day was as follows.

On the night of the first evening, I recall we all went out for dinner in Porto and had the most extraordinary fish stew. I remember the prawns being of what seemed like gigantic proportions compared to what we saw in the UK. The wine during the meal was Peter Bright's Dry Muscat, a real Portuguese innovation at the time.

I remember getting into a conversation with Paul Symington about the various quintas (farms, or chateaus in equivalent) the company was involved with, and he happened to mention Quinta do Bom Retiro. I immediately piped up wasn't that a brand that belonged to the port house Ramos Pinto. To which he replied, "You have got a brain like a computer!"- which I took as a backhanded compliment. I was right, but as he went on to explain half of the vineyard belonged to the Serôdio family who had supplied their grapes for Warre's port for many years, and Ramos Pinto purchased the other for their brand. Since 2006 the Serôdio vineyard has been owned by the Symington family. I think (rightly!) we ended the meal with Smith Woodhouse 'Old Lodge' tawny port.

Paul Symington at the stunning railway station in Porto.

The second day was with Paul Symington to a new warehouse complex they had just built for bottling, labelling, and storage of all their brands, a visit to the Factory House, (which is where the picture of us holding the bottles was taken) and in the afternoon with both he and Bill Warre we travelled up by train to the Douro to stay at Quinta do Bomfim. Here we met several other members of the family who were all very hospitable. The house had a wonderful colonial feel about it and had been built by Bill Warre's relative George Warre in 1896.

I remember being at the dinner table with Michael Symington at the head and me sitting to his left, with Amyas, Peter, and other family members and he asking me if

I smoked cigars! They didn't agree with him so he didn't and I replied only at Christmas (which was true - but only one!).

That evening we visited Quinta da Cavadinha which was still using stone lagars and here was a chance to tread the grapes. I must admit I was a bit concerned at first as I remember thinking if I get grape must all over my shirt how on earth will I get it out? Silly when you look back now, but I don't think I brought many shirts with me for the trip! Michael Chewter persuaded me to step into the lagar so I did and away we went, and thoroughly enjoyed the experience! This was also the first time Johnny Symington had stepped into a lagar!

Treading the grapes at Quinta da Cavadinha. I cannot recall the names of the two gentlemen in the photograph (to the left) but Johnny Symington is in the red shorts with me Michael Chewter and Peter Symington to the right.

Getting some sort of rhythm going. The result of our efforts is somewhere within the Warre's 1985 Vintage Port!

The shirt was indeed splattered with wine must stain, and before retiring to bed I had been told to just drop my shirt in the middle of the room and leave it at that. In the morning, to my amazement there was the shirt, cleaned, ironed, and neatly folded as if new sitting ready on a chair! I was extremely grateful to the staff at Bomfim for their help.

On the third day, we visited various quintas in the morning to see the wines being made and were driven by Peter Symington with Johnny along hair-raising bends and drops and spectacular views of the valleys. We returned to Porto by train later that day and back to London on the following. It had been a remarkable trip.

On our way to visit the quintas.

Breaking up the cap of skins, pips and stems with 'Monkeys' at Quinta das Lages. Large wooden paddles to help the fermentation.

Drawing the wine off the lees.

The storage vats at Quinta das Lages, with 'W/J Graham' on the vat blackboard.

Being presented at the Factory House, with Bill Warre to the left, myself, Michael Chewter and Ian Symington.

~~~~~~~~~~

AN UNEASY ALLIANCE

Now it was back to the job at André Simon Wines. I would meet many interesting people over this period and was very fortunate. Certain personalities who stood out were Maria Canning of Matthew Clark who was charming; Tim Stanley Clarke from Fells who was always a lively engaging personality, plus many more of course.

I also recall a gentleman from Seagram's who would always turn his pictorial product booklet toward me and slowly turn each page and explain what lines they had. His was an extremely monotone in his delivery, almost sedate, and I used to think that he really didn't enjoy his job at all!

One particular visit from a representative I do remember with James present was a gentleman who represented a large selection of French wines, predominately Chateau wines. Whilst Chateau Cheval Blanc was a renowned 1st Grand Cru Classe, he however had Chateau Cheval Noire, whose virtues he extolled! His polished oratory seemed to go on for some time and he was clearly very knowledgeable. At the end of it all after he left James used an expression I had never heard before "he (the gentleman) knew his onions" which still makes me smile.

Not all was plain sailing however, and the introduction of new lines by James was receiving lukewarm enthusiasm from the shop managers. Whether they had decided to take a stance on this from the very beginning as a collective group to block Ray Gough's initiative or felt James's presence was unwarranted, I do not know. But, they would not make it easy.

Perhaps they also had a point in as much as their shops (all located in affluent locations) normally catered for the 'traditional' wine customer who frequented their stores, brought up on champagne, claret, burgundy and so forth. Would they even be interested in what went on in the rest of the wine world?

Either way, it was a difficult period, and I was more than aware of the antipathy. Come what may I was going to make the best of my time there.

Much along the lines of Cullen's James had organised a public tasting to introduce many of these new lines at a location in the west end to show the range. The turnout was disappointingly low, but in his true resilient fashion he said "we will get them in in time".

James did carry out tastings in store, and perhaps won over one or two of the more enlightened managers and staff, but it was an uneasy alliance.

My trips over to James's offices in Lambeth would also involve scrutinising the André Simon list. One occasion I do recall is when we were discussing the fine wine Claret list. My pronunciation of Château Ducru Beaucaillou was a tangled contorted affair and caused some amusement, and we both laughed along together!

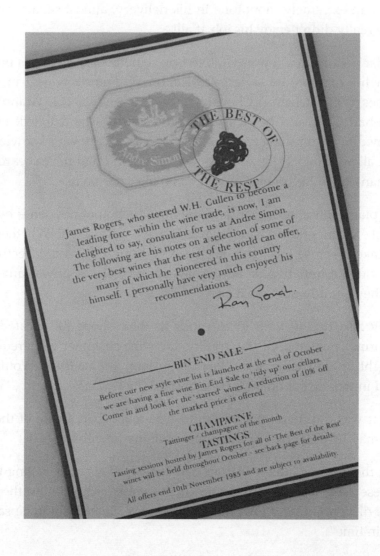

THE BEST OF THE REST

James Rogers, who steered W.H. Cullen to become a leading force within the wine trade, is now, I am delighted to say, consultant for us at Andre Simon. The following are his notes on a selection of some of the very best wines that the rest of the world can offer, many of which he pioneered in this country himself. I personally have very much enjoyed his recommendations.

Ray Gonal.

•

BIN END SALE

Before our new style wine list is launched at the end of October we are having a fine wine Bin End Sale to 'tidy up' our cellars. Come in and look for the 'starred' wines. A reduction of 10% off the marked price is offered.

CHAMPAGNE
Taittinger - champagne of the month

TASTINGS

Tasting sessions hosted by James Rogers for all of 'The Best of the Rest' wines will be held throughout October - see back page for details.

All offers end 10th November 1985 and are subject to availability.

From the first wine offer pamphlet produced after joining André Simon, and announcing James arrival.

BEST OF THE REST

The great advancement of Wine technology in the last 20 years has brought about a revolution in wine-making. Although France still produces the finest wine 'experiences' that the fermented grape can muster, other countries can often outstrip them in quality and value for money. This is particularly apparent in wines in the lower and middle price brackets. Over the past 5 years I have pioneered some of these wines and am delighted to be able to introduce them to you now.

AUSTRALIA

'As good as California - at half the price!'

BROWN BROS
KOOMBAHLA 'CABERNET SAUVIGNON 1981
A superb example of the power and yet finesse that an
Australian red wine can produce. Top New World
Cabernets produce these 'Cassis-like' minty flavours. £6.80

ROSEMOUNT CHARDONNAY 1984
Here is a fine example of how an Australian
Chardonnay can match up to, and indeed beat the
French equivalent in this price bracket.
A soft round wine with classic lemony acidity. £4.95

HILL SMITH BAROSSA VALLEY RIESLING 1985
This has Germanic grapey fruit but French dryness.
A very good aperitif and first course wine. £3.45

NEW ZEALAND

I wrote in the 1981 Which Wine? Guide that New Zealand would be competing with France in quality within 5 years. Selaks Sauvignon Blanc (soon to be exclusive to André Simon) has just won the What Wine? Sauvignon tasting against the rest of the worlds top Sauvignons. Whilst waiting for this wine to arrive in this country we offer the one placed second.

MONTANA SAUVIGNON BLANC 1982
Very classical gooseberry flavours.
Recently voted a top rated wine in What Wine? Magazine. £3.95

CHILE

This country has been exporting wines to this country for over 30 years. Their reds are widely acknowledged to be superior to their whites.

COUSINO MACUL 1978
Another 100% Cabernet Sauvignon (Bordeaux grape).
Full, rich, with again blackcurrent overtones. £4.35

Content from the pamphlet, introducing wines that were to become staples on the UK market.

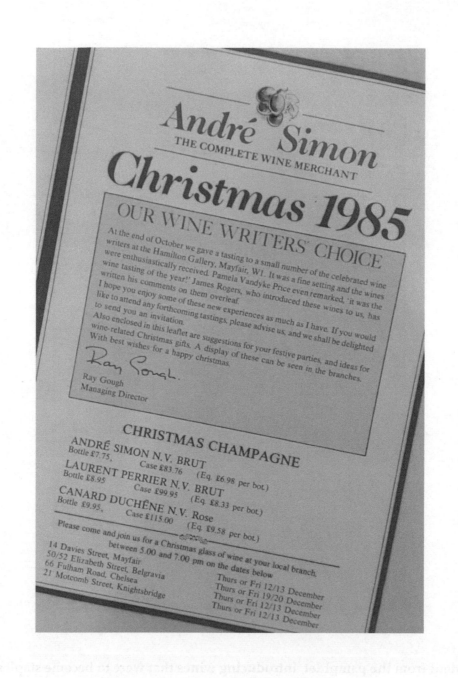

The Christmas pamphlet from the same year.

PORT IN A STORM

In November 1986 I had a letter printed in Decanter Magazine which caused a bit of a stir. It was in response to a tasting of Single Quinta ports which had appeared in the May edition and my thoughts on the subject. It was simply a case of pointing out various facts as I saw them, and received some interesting reactions. Colin Parnell the editor was supportive, and I remember Dominic Symington calling in to see me at André Simon, who was also very interested. I was happy enough with the piece.

A further reaction from it was from Julian Brind MW, a wine buyer at Waitrose, who invited me along to see him at their head office in Bracknell to discuss the article. It was a slightly strange affair as I remember we met in the staff canteen along with other wine buyers simply around a table eating their lunch. He referend to the article of course but I was taken aback by his comment, "did someone pay you to write this?" To which I replied, "of course not". I have to say that I did take this as a bit of an affront, and why on earth he saw it from that viewpoint I will never know. I was disappointed by his comment but shrugged it off. If this had been what he wanted to know perhaps he could have saved me the journey and just asked me over the phone.

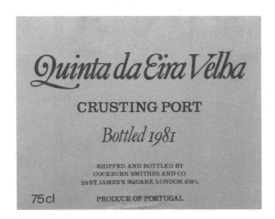

One of the examples referred to in the article was this 'Single Quinta' Crusting Port produced by Cockburn's.

Single Quinta vintage ports

AFTER READING your report on *Single Quinta* Ports in the May edition of *Decanter Magazine*, I was intrigued in the selection of wines chosen for the tasting, and would like to make the following comments.

If a true comparison of 'Single Quinta' ports was to be made, then should not the tasting have been as comprehensive as possible and as many wines from all the currently available vintages and shippers have been included, to be able to draw any positive conclusions as to quality? I assume that price was not a criteria as there was no mention of a ceiling price for the tasting itself — although a 'Guide Price' of between £10 and £12 was given, presumably as an average to expect to pay. This being so, I could not understand why the wines of Offley's Boa Vista 1982 and '83 were included in the tasting, but not eh Offley vintages of '63, '66, '70, '75, '77 and '80. Many of these vintages are stocked by wine merchants around the country, and I am sure that if they had been included they would have produced interesting results.

The lack of presence of 'Quinta do Noval' — possibly the most famous 'Single Quinta' port of all, I found most puzzling, especially as Noval '78 was included in the 'Single Quinta' Port Tasting in the Decanter issue of October 1982 — so why not here again?

I was also interested in Elizabeth Berry's comment that she would not stock Single Quinta ports. Perhaps the fact that Sainsbury's were selling Graham's Malvedos 1968 at an incredibly low price has some bearing on this, and I would imagine, for the sake of harmony within the trade, that this is unlikely to happen again.

May I also say that Colin Parnell's claim — that Graham's Malvedos no longer carried the 'Quinta' name — is incorrect. In fact it never did. The word 'Quinta' has never appeared on the main label, even when the company was owned by the Graham family prior to the Symington take-over in 1970. It follows that Graham's Malvedos is not solely the product of the 'Quinta' alone but is blended with wines from adjacent vineyards — and often wrongly sold as Graham's 'Quinta dos Malvedos'.

Finally, I would like to add that although the Decanter verdict was that 'Singel Quinta' ports should not be declared in classic years, the wines of Offley Boa Vista and Quinta do Noval have always been declared and, technically, they are 'Single Quinta' wines — how do they stand?

Clearly new legislation is required to clarify the situation for the consumer. The terminology 'Single Quinta' has no legal standing as such, and can be used freely as it is now, for both Vintage and Tawny Ports, such as Ramos-Pinto's, Quinta do Bom-Retiro 20 year old. Even a 'Single Quinta Crusting Port' exists in the form of Quinta do Eira Velha, shipped by Cockburn's.

Perhaps the term 'Second Wine' Vintage Port may well be a better description — similar to the 'Second Wines' produced by Cru classé properties in Bordeaux — and could cover both Single Vineyard Ports such as Taylor's Vargellas and also blended wines such as Graham's Malvedos — but both only released in undeclared years.

The final contradiction to all this must to to Croft & Co, when they released a Croft's 'Quinta do Roeda' Vintage Port as well as a 'declared' Croft Vintage Port in the same year — 1970.

Brian Gates,
Hampton,
Middlesex.

Colin Parnell comments: Yes, it *is* confusing. Although *Quinta do Noval* is a single quinta vintage port, its producers consider it to be a 'classical', top quality wine and on this occasion did not wish it to be included among the 'ordinary' single quinta ports.

The name of the company producing Noval ports is 'Quinta do Noval — Vinhos SARL', and their wines do not necessarily come exclusively from the vineyard of the same name. The company used to be called 'Antonio José de Silva Lda' and then Noval was apparently a single quinta wine.

It's true that the main label of *Graham's Malvedos Vintage Port* makes no mention of the word 'quinta', but the back label does: 'Grahams Quinta dos Malvedos is one of the finest vineyard properties in the Alto Douro', it states, and goes on to add, 'Most years produce at least a small amount of top-class Port and the exceptionally fine wines of Malvedos are bottled when two years old, as is traditional Vintage Port.'

The implication of such wording is that the wine comes entirely from the quinta. But, strictly speaking, the label does not actually say so. In fact, it comes from the quinta and neighbouring vineyards.

The article that appeared in Decanter Magazine in November 1986.

100

CHANGES ONCE MORE

As we moved into 1987 it became evident that changes were underway. Unbeknown to any of us (except those closest to him) Mr. Gough had decided to sell the business.

The new buyer would be Graham Chidgey of Layton's. It was a strange day indeed when Mr. Chidgey visited the shop at Davies Street and asked to go through the buying terms André Simon had on their lines. I of course obliged, and in some instances, the terms the company had on costs from suppliers were extremely good. It felt like handing over state secrets!

For me personally, this presented a dilemma, as clearly I would no longer be required as they had their own buying team and James's consultancy would naturally come to an end. The four shops would all now go under the Jeroboam umbrella.

What disappointed me most was the way in which it had been done. It was Mr. Gough's prerogative to do what he wished of course, but somehow some indication of what was to occur would have given me more time to look for a new employer. Consequently, now, my back was against the wall.

I had no option but to look for a new position during my working hours at André Simon, and since I was under redundancy notice if that meant I had to leave the office and go, I would. The atmosphere now was uneasy, tense and I think Mr. Gough was more concerned about what I might say to a potential new employer about my experiences of working for him than anything else, but this never happened and I never discussed it.

I had met many people over this period, and many were sympathetic to what had occurred, but the true test would be in what would happen next.

As I travelled home with James in his car one evening during this period he said to me now at least I had made 'contacts' in the trade, which was true enough, but converting that into gainful employment was something else.

Although almost two years had passed since Jane Hunt had worked for André Simon Wines she still made the occasional visit to Davies Street and was now working for Walter Siegel & Co Ltd.

Siegel's at this time had the Brown Brothers Australian agency and had made great strides with the brand. They were extremely busy and had been looking for a manager to handle things in the office (which would encompass several other duties) and she would put my name forward to Nigel Blundell the MD.

Ironically, Walter Siegel was now located at 50 Battersea Park Road so not far from where I had previously worked for Cullen's.

Whilst I waited to hear on this I was also looking at other options and one interview I did have was with Mentzendorff & Co who were then located at Great Peter Street, but the interview with two of its Directors took place in a hotel in central London. Both gentlemen were very pleasant and the interview went well. I visited Great Peter Street and met the office staff there and the position was mine if I chose to take it. I had little experience of using computers up until this point (which Mentzendorff had) and this made me a little uneasy about the post, but I was sure I would pick it up quickly.

I also received a call from Nigel Blundell during this period and went to see him in Battersea. As mentioned previously I had met Nigel originally whilst in the Cullen head office in the early 1980s and he was always friendly and engaging. He too offered me the position and the problem now was which one to accept. Having weighed things up I decided to go with Nigel.

Before the end at André Simon's Tim Stanley Clarke of Fells was good enough to invite me on a trip to the Douro once more. Robert Joseph was amongst the group and very good company, and although it was jolly, for me it was perhaps a change of role yet again at the back of my mind that led me to enjoy it less. Nevertheless, I was grateful for the opportunity of course and to see Paul Symington and the extended family once more.

This overlapped with me joining Walter Siegel so on my return went straight into work there.

WALTER S. SIEGEL Ltd

Although the address for Walter Siegel was 50 Battersea Park Road, the entrance to the offices was just off the main road in Cupar Road. The offices were in effect a flat above a shop, underneath of which was Jason's Restaurant. Nigel Blundell was also part owner of the restaurant, with a gentleman called Costas, and once Nigel's day job at Siegel's was over he would then go on to work in the restaurant.

In terms of staff at Siegel's, there was along with Nigel, John Boys, Jane and Ian Gerard Pearce one of the reps. John Boys was always very affable, and one of the earliest MWs and had a desk on the top floor with Nigel, as did Jane. Next to them was a second room which contained a fairly large oval table and a sink for tasting which overlooked an alleyway off Cupar Road.

My office was on the level below, next to which was an office with the two other ladies. There was a small room at the far end to store wines, and contained numerous samples, predominately Brown Brothers. I often wondered about the sheer weight on the floor itself! But this really was a converted flat for office purposes.

One thing that did attract me to the job at Siegel's was the Australian connection of the Brown Brothers agency and the Rutherglen Muscat's. Australian wines had made great headway, and Nigel had worked hard and it had paid off. Along with Rosemount Wines (represented by Mike Rayment in the UK), these two wineries were really seen at the time as being the pinnacle of what Australia had to offer for export and was enjoying huge popularity - and sales.

The fortified Australian Muscat's were also fascinating wines, informally referred to as 'stickies' they had a charm and character unlike anything else.

Once again Jane showed me the ropes of the job, how the costings were put together for the wholesale wines, how the containers were arranged for shipment from Australia, the bonding arrangements, plus several other aspects. It was very different to what I had done at André Simon's, but the company had a good feel about it and vibrancy no doubt brought about by the success of the Australian wines.

Then, within two weeks of joining disaster struck, news came through that Siegel's were to lose the Brown Brother's agency. For Nigel who had put so much effort into this, it was a terrible blow and seemed almost inconceivable. But that was the case and it was to go to a new agent.

ALL THE EGGS...

The most worrying aspect of this was the amount of lost trade this would represent to Siegel's. Although they had several other agencies they were nothing in comparison to Brown Brothers, and the balance was tipped very much that way, accounting for perhaps 90 per cent of the company's business. It was not a good situation to be in.

The news not unnaturally came as a shock to all concerned and an unsettling air now replaced that spirit I had experienced when I first arrived.

I remember saying to Nigel if he was considering in making me redundant could he please at least give me a couple of months' notice?!

After a few weeks, the shock of losing Brown Brothers had calmed but the future seemed very uncertain. But, given how effective Siegel's had been in selling the wine a decision was made to look for a new Australian agency to replace it.

As the search began and enquiries made to various other Australian wineries it was discovered that Seppelt's wines, which were being represented by the Eldridge Pope Brewery in Dorset at the time, were selling as little as 500 cases a year. They appeared to be an ideal candidate to follow up further and the search was on to find some of their wines in London to sample the quality. I remember Jane heading out to an independent wine merchant and returning with three or four bottles from their Black Label range, but it was still all very hush-hush.

The quality was good so Seppelt's were approached, and the agency eventually, after a wait changed hands. I remember the day the news came through that Siegel's had got the agency was one of great relief and to celebrate Nigel arranged a meal for the staff downstairs in the restaurant!

Just before this occurred however Ian Gerard Pearce had decided he wished to move on and left, and not long after securing the agency Jane had decided it was time for her to leave also.

Various samples of Seppelt's wines started to arrive from Australia including their Moyston/Queen Adelaide blends, the obligatory red and white varietals, and Seppelt's Great Western sparkling wine which was a big brand in Australia, plus their fortified wines. Being such a large producer their range was fairly eclectic, and all labels of course would need to be rejigged to comply with the UK and refined in design. It would be a question of what wines would work best in this market.

These were still uncertain times and it would take a lot of work and time to get Seppelt's volumes up from such small quantities. With a smaller staff now there would naturally be a lot to do, and it would require all of Nigel's experience.

One morning, not long after arriving at Siegel's I remember Nigel telling me that James Rogers had come to have a meal at his restaurant the night before and was pleased that I had found a position with him. He had also told Nigel that I had a very good palate, which coming from James was quite a compliment.

THE TRADE SHOWS

One of the highlights of working at Siegel's for me was the trade tastings (and on one occasion, a public tasting!) I remember the first one I ever went to with Siegel's was with John Boys in the very earliest days of having the Seppelt agency. I can't recall exactly where it was but we only had one wine! It was a small stock of Seppelt's Oak Matured Barooga Chardonnay. Very much in the style of the day, it was fairly heavily oaked but smooth and rich, we all thought it was a good wine.

With one wine you didn't need much of a stand and it was tiny! Poor John Boys looked a bit fed up with it all and I remember him sitting at the stand table with his hands clasped under his chin and his head resting on them with his angled elbows on the table. For me it was a bit of a novelty, but for John Boys perhaps not so! But, to our complete surprise, the Seppelt Chardonnay won a Gold Medal at the show, along with one other well-established Australian wine brand then, Lindeman's Bin 65. I remember a lady from the Lindeman's stand coming over to us and sportingly congratulating us on the wine's success which she felt was well deserved. This gave us all some real encouragement as to the quality Seppelt's possessed commercially.

Another trade show that stands out in my mind (for perhaps all the wrong reasons!) was the Australia Day tasting on the 27th January 1988 at the Lord's cricket ground. On this occasion, it was the Rutherglen Muscat agencies that were to be the represented of which Siegel's had four producers.

Being that this was Australia's 200th Anniversary it was decided that as well as the trade tasting during the day it would be open to the public in the evening. I was really looking forward to the event and in my suit made my way to Lord's in anticipation. Coming out of the tube station close to Lord's the weather suddenly opened up into a downpour of biblical proportions, and in what seemed like just seconds I was completely drenched through, and looked more like a drowned rat!

Once I arrived at Lord's I immediately made my way to the gentleman's toilet and in a cubicle, in disbelief, poured out the contents of my shoes which were full of water. I then had to wring out my socks also into the bowl!

From here I made my way up to the trade tasting floor and spent the rest of the day relying on my body heat to do the best it could in drying out the clothes, which was not much!

I remember that such were the wind gusts that morning that the large window panes of glass on the stand floor at Lord's creaked and flexed from the intensity of the wind as it howled and whipped around the building.

In the evening the public (especially the ladies!) loved the Liqueur Muscat's, and our table was extremely busy, it had been quite a day…

The big wine trade show of the period was of course the London Wine Trade Fair at Olympia. I recall we would often get visits to the Siegel stand from managers of retailers, such as Oddbins, some of whom would ask how you could get into the wholesale side of the trade. It reminded me of my earliest days in the trade and the advice I was once given.

FROM SMALL BEGINNINGS

Once the initial Seppelt range was finalised for the UK market a container was put together, and it would naturally be a slow start to get the wines established. One of my jobs was to arrange the container shipments and liaise with Seppelt's in Australia. We would also add small parcels of the Liqueur Muscat's and incorporate them into the shipments. All the paperwork for the imports had to be spot on, otherwise, delays could take place which could end up being costly, and so getting the finer details right was important. Once it arrived in the UK it would be bonded and released as required. I dealt with all the paperwork concerning this, having a separate file for each shipment. It was a 14,000-mile journey from Australia so getting the container timings right for departures and deliveries was important.

It is interesting to see how technology was changing so rapidly even then. I always thought the Telex machine was a marvellous invention only then to be superseded by the Fax machine.

I remember in those early Seppelt days we were cost conscious and any communication with Seppelt's in Australia was sent by fax after the office was closed and the timer set. Partly as it was cheaper, and the other point was that Australia was ten hours ahead so they would be ready to get going on the instructions first thing. Nigel would sometimes have copious amounts of A4 pages ready to send. The only problem in doing it out of hours is that if there was a paper jam they didn't get the whole story!

The two people we dealt with on a daily basis then were Maggie Hanratty the Export Co-ordinator at Seppelt's and Freddie Choong the International Operation's Manager. They were extremely tolerant and helpful in many ways and we had developed a good working relationship.

Whilst the shipping element of the job was important of course, what I really enjoyed was the chance to get involved in some design work and in particular the wholesale wine list. In line with the cost consciousness of the time, I put it to Nigel that I could design the list layout and set about cutting and pasting bits and bobs, taking elements of design from here and there, and putting it all together. There was no computer then so it was all done by hand. As I look at the results now, some thirty-three years later, it doesn't look like too bad a job really!

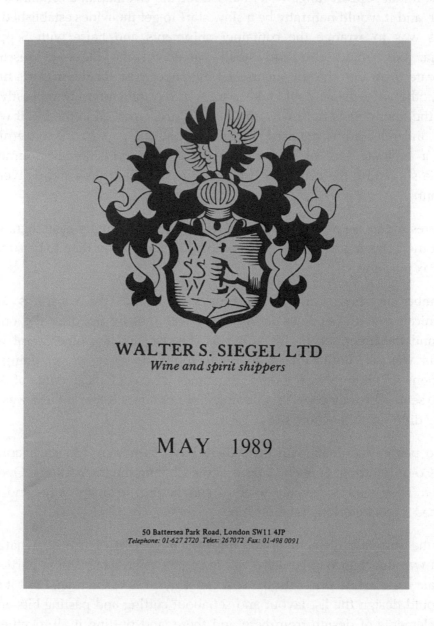

WALTER S. SIEGEL LTD
Wine and spirit shippers

MAY 1989

50 Battersea Park Road, London SW11 4JP
Telephone: 01-627 2720 Telex: 267072 Fax: 01-498 0091

THE HOUSE OF
SEPPELT

	DPO PRICES		
	25-50 CASES	12-24 CASES	6-11 CASES
MOYSTON RANGE			
Moyston Red, Shiraz/Cabernet Sauvignon 1986	£32.10	£32.75	£33.75
Moyston Dry White, Semillon 1987	32.10	32.75	33.75
Moyston Medium Dry White 1987	32.10	32.75	33.75
GOLD LABEL RANGE			
Semillon/Chardonnay 1987/88	38.00	38.75	40.00
Shiraz/Cabernet 1985/86	41.35	42.20	43.50
Chardonnay Non Oaked 1988	43.60	44.50	45.85
Cabernet Sauvignon 1985/86	45.50	46.40	47.80
BLACK LABEL AND PREMIUM RANGE			
Cabernet Sauvignon Black Label 1985/86	52.95	54.10	55.75
Shiraz Black Label 1985	52.95	54.10	55.75
Chardonnay, Oak Matured 1988	48.45	50.00	51.50
Premier Vineyard Selection Cabernet/Malbec 1983	65.10	66.45	68.50
SPARKLING			
Great Western Imperial Reserve N.V.	41.75	42.60	43.90
Great Western Rose Brut N.V.	41.75	42.60	43.90
Great Western Chardonnay Brut 1986/87	59.00	60.20	62.00
FORTIFIED			
Mt. Rufus, Finest Tawny (average 5 years)	55.80	57.00	58.75
Rutherglen Show Muscat D.P. 63			
(packed 12 to case)	83.50	85.25	87.90

STANTON & KILLEEN
"GRACERRAY" WINERY

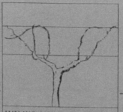

WINES OF RUTHERGLEN

ALL SAINTS VINEYARD

THE RUTHERGLEN LIQUEUR MUSCAT COLLECTION

We are now representing five of the finest Rutherglen growers, who produce the best Liqueur Muscats to be found in Australia. Often matured in wood for many years, they start life with a reddish tinge maturing to dark brown with olive-green hues on the rim. They have wonderful complexities of flavour and can be enjoyed at any time.

		DPD PRICES 25-50 CASES	12-24 CASES	6-11 CASES
ALL SAINTS RUTHERGLEN				
Liqueur Muscat	Per 6 Bottles	£34.90	£35.60	£36.70
Premium Liqueur Muscat	" " " "	39.05	39.85	41.10
STANTON & KILLEEN OF RUTHERGLEN				
Liqueur Muscat	Per 6 Bottles	34.90	35.60	36.70
W.H. CHAMBERS OF RUTHERGLEN				
Liqueur Muscat	Per 6 Bottles	31.80	32.50	33.50
Special Liqueur Muscat	" " " "	56.80	57.95	59.75
Old Liqueur Muscat (Limited release)	" " " "	160.55	163.95	169.00
CAMPBELLS OF RUTHERGLEN				
Liqueur Muscat (Gift Packed)	Per 6 Bottles	34.90	35.60	36.70
Old Rutherglen Liqueur Muscat (Gift Packed)	Per 6 Bottles	47.40	48.40	49.90
Rutherglen Shiraz Table Wine 1985	Per 12 Bottles	46.40	47.40	48.85
B. SEPPELT & SONS LIMITED				
Rutherglen Show Muscat D.P. 63	Per 12 Bottles	83.50	85.25	87.90

CAMPBELLS WINERY

CHAMBERS ROSEWOOD WINERY

Whilst I had been at André Simon Wines with James I had come up with the idea of funding the cost of the print run of their glossy wine catalogue by asking suppliers if they wanted to advertise their label's within it. Several suppliers agreed and the cost would be £200 per label inclusion. In the end, it raised something in the region of £1,200 which more than covered the catalogue costs. So I had also been involved in the design aspect back then.

The sparkling wine element within the Seppelt range also opened up other possibilities which the Brown Brothers range hadn't. Australian wines were very big at this time in the UK of course, and the premium wine within the Seppelt sparkling range was Salinger, which was eventually shipped over, along with a sparkling red Shiraz which was a real novelty at the time. I also suggested to Nigel that 'own label' sparkling wine was another possibility and he put the offer to Tesco who took up the opportunity.

It was satisfying to see after a few years the growth of the Seppelt wines, and I remember the day we were told exports to the UK had reached 150,000 cases and we all felt a sense of achievement.

THE SANDEMAN PEACE PIPE

My interest in port wine however never left me and again I had a letter appear in Decanter Magazine on the subject. On this occasion, it included some confusion over vintage years for both vintage ports and LBV's, and I made a reference to Sandeman's 1978 Vintage Port. The following month a reply appeared in the magazine from David Sandeman stating that they had not released a 1978 vintage port as I had written in my article. The only problem was that I had a label of the 1978 Vintage Port - as supplied to me by Sandeman's!

As the mini spat went on various telex messages went back and forth to Portugal and as I explained I was sent the label over two years earlier - by them. The explanation as to what had happened then finally came through from a less than happy Mr. Sandeman that the label should never have been sent out in the first place!

They had produced a vintage port that year, but only one pipe, which was intended to mark the birth of his first grandson. It transpired that a former employee had sent the label out and that Mr. Sandeman was unaware that a label had even been produced for what was meant to be a 'private bottling'.

The upside to all this was that rather than have it ping back and forth in the magazine he wanted to make a peace offering and arranged to send over from Portugal six bottles of the said port for me - with the now overlaid 'private bottling' applied to the label. I was happy to accept of course and make both the bottles, and the original label, fairly rare I imagine.

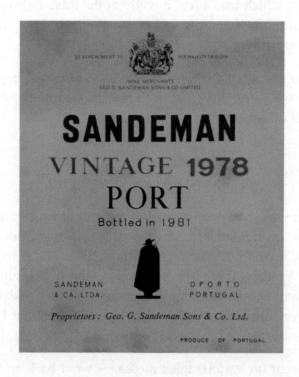

The original Sandeman label that caused the commotion.

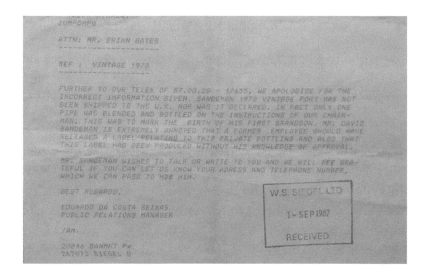

The reply from Sandman's finally explained what had occurred, and the now overlaid 'Private Bottling' applied to the label (below).

DR. LOOSEN BREAKTHROUGH

Both John Boys and Nigel had a love of German wines of course, but at this point in time sales of high-quality German wines were extremely low, and difficult to sell. But there was one producer whose passion and determination stood out, and that was Ernst Loosen.

Nigel relayed the story that Ernst had tried nearly every wine agent in the UK phone directory before hitting upon Siegel's, and up until then had been given short thrift. John Boys, however, who had served in the army in World War Two as an Intelligence Officer, greeted Ernst in his native tongue on the telephone and was more than happy to help. As it turned out this was a good move, and Ernst showcased his wines at a tasting in London I recall, and the quality shone through!

THE WHICH? PORT TASTING

In August 1989 John Boys had received an invitation to take part in a Which? Port tasting and had passed the opportunity over to me given my interest. What I particularly liked about the idea is that it was an opportunity to meet with Bill Warre once more, but there had been no indication as to the number of wines to be sampled. It was being held by Roger Voss in central London and I made my way there by tube.

When I arrived and saw the tasting list was comprised of some 46 ports! With the best will in the world of both sampling and spitting out the contents, this would be a challenge! Undaunted, I and the other judges headed into the fray, but by about halfway through the difficulty in tasting so many in an objective manner became clear. With discipline applied I made sure I did not swallow any of the samples, but this of course (being port wine) did not mean it was not lining my mouth! As we came to the end of the tasting and deliberated it was eventually time to head back to work. I remember saying farewell to Bill Warre on the platform of the tube station before the journey back, but feeling both slightly inebriated and my head in a real spin! I cannot remember anything else about the journey, but like a homing pigeon found my way back in one piece.

Wednesday 13 September 1989

£

Vintage Character

1) Fine Old VC, Smith Woodhouse (Thresher)   5.99
2) Asda Fine Old Port VC, Smith Woodhouse (Asda)   4.69
3) Old Treaty VC, Martinez Gassiot (Victoria Wine Company   5.39
4) Berry's VC, Taylors (Berry Bros)   8.40
5) Fine Old VC, Royal Oporto (Tesco)   4.69
6) Cassons Fine Old VC, Smith Woodhouse (Co-op)   5.19
7) Adnams VC, Martinez Gassiot (Adnams)   6.75
8) Marks & Spencer VC, Morgan Bros (Marks & Spencer)   5.99
9) Sainsbury's Fine Old VC, Taylors (Sainsbury's)   4.99
10) Fonseca Bin No 27 VC (Mentzendorff)   7.40
11) Churchill's VC (Churchill Graham)   approx 7.75
12) Grahams Six Grapes VC (Matthew Clark)   approx 7.30
13) Warre's Warrior Port (John E Fells)   6.99
14) Gould Campbell VC (Lawlers)   (only available in restaurants)
15) Dow's VC (John E Fells)   6.99
16) Delaforce Fine Rich VC (Dent & Reuss)   6.99
17) Ramos-Pinto VC (Berkmann)   6.45
18) Calem VC (Wine Growers Association)   6.80
19) Sandeman VC (Seagram)   approx 5.99
20) Royal Oporto VC (T J Keats)   approx 5.50
21) De Souza VC (Richmond Wine Warehouse)   6.50

Late-Bottled Vintage

22) Noval LB (Sichel)   approx 6.00
23) Chairman's LBV (Eldridge Pope)   6.96
24) Royal Oporto 1985 LBV (T J Keats)   approx 7.50
25) Taylor's 1984 LBV (Deinhard)   8.99
26) Tesco 1984 LBV, Smith Woodhouse (Tesco)   5.99
27) Marks & Spencer 1983 LBV, Morgan Bros (Marks & Spencer)   8.99
28) Fonseca 1983 LBV (Mentzendorff)   8.30
29) Robertson's Rebello Valente 1983 LBV (Laytons)   6.65
30) Delaforce 1983 LBV (Dent & Reuss)   7.99
31) Ramos-Pinto 1983 LBV (Berkmann)   7.35
32) Croft 1983 LBV (Percy Fox)   14.49
33) Calem 1983 LBV (Wine Growers Association)   7.70
34) Sandeman 1983 LBV (Seagram)   approx 7.50
35) Sainsbury's 1983 LBV, Temilobos (Sainsbury's)   5.75
36) Asda Own-label 1982 LBV (Asda)   5.99
37) Cockburns 1982 LBV (Victoria Wine Company)   7.29
38) Offley 1982 LBV (Rutherford, Osborne & Perkins)   approx 7.75
39) De Souza 1982 LBV (Richmond Wine Warehouse)   7.75
40) Grahams 1982 LBV (Matthew Clark)   approx 6.99
41) Gould Campbell 1982 LBV (Lawlers)   (available only in restaurants)
42) Dow's Port 1982 LBV (John E Fells)   6.79
43) Niepoort 1982 LBV (Peake Wine Associates)   6.55
44) Kopke 1982 LBV (Hayward Bros)   7.69
45) Smith Woodhouse 1979 LBV (John E Fells)   11.25
46) Niepoort 1975 LBV (Peake Wine Associates)   8.04

The wines tasted that day to determine the quality of both Vintage Character and Late bottled Vintage Ports.

WHICH? WINE MONTHLY

EDITORS: AILEEN HALL AND ROGER VOSS

30 OCT 1989

VINTAGE CONFUSION IN PORTS

Vintage port is the finest expression of style and character that a port producer can make. But it is expensive: it can be made only in great years and even then only in limited quantities.

One of the notable advances in recent years has been the way that port producers have started to offer less expensive substitutes for true vintage port, a boon for anyone who likes a bottle on the go over Christmas. These alternatives come in two styles and most producers produce both: Vintage Character (VC) and Late Bottled Vintage (LBV).

For many purists, both styles are pale substitutes of the real thing. Unlike vintage ports, which age in bottle for many years, VCs and LBVs are designed to be drunk within a few years of the harvest. To achieve this, they are matured in wood for longer than the maximum two years for a vintage port, and then, generally, pasteurised to stop any further development of the wine before being sold and drunk.

They are not vintage port, certainly. But, as our tasting showed, some very enjoyable wines are around. However, it also showed that – in both categories – there is a great deal of confusion about how producers regard VCs and LBVs, and therefore equal – or greater – confusion on the part of the drinking public.

The regulations covering VCs and LBVs are at the same time specific and vague. The rules for LBVs, for example, state that approval must be given by the governing body of port, the Instituto do Vinho do Porto, set down when the wine should be bottled (any time between four and six years after the harvest), stipulate the need for a guarantee seal over the cork when

Our tasters this month were: Chris Foulkes, managing editor of wine books at publishers Mitchell Beazley; Brian Gates of wine shippers Walter Siegel; John Thorogood of wine merchants Lay & Wheeler; William Warre MW, of the port family, who works at John E Fells; Nicholas Wright of wine merchants Berry Bros & Rudd; and *Which? Wine Monthly*'s joint editor, Roger Voss. (As always, the wines were tasted blind; and marks of any taster whose company had supplied a sample were discounted for that wine.)

HOUSE OF COMMONS SOIRÉE

A further occasion I recall is when Walter Siegel had won an award and it was to be presented at the House of Commons. I cannot remember exactly what it was for but it turned out that neither Nigel nor John Boys could make it so that left me. Being that this was a prestigious occasion a morning suit was called for, something I naturally did not own. John Boys however said that he did have one packed away somewhere and that I was welcome to use it if it fitted. Well, when he brought it in it was clearly of some age, perhaps even having belonged to his father! I tried it on and it was of a heavy woollen fabric so had considerable weight, but looked more as if it had come out of the Boar War era! I looked more like I was auditioning for an Edwardian melodrama! I remember it caused much laughter in the office at the time.

In the end, my uncle supplied me with an appropriate bow tie and suit for the occasion, so all was well.

A young man called Grant Page had also joined the sales team at Siegel's during this time. Grant was from Australia and he had an English wife who ran a shop, The Lemon Tree in York Road, Battersea I seem to recall. Whether he was asked to join the sales team at the request of Seppelt's in Australia I am unsure.

ANTIPODEAN OVERSEAS VISITORS

One of the more pleasurable aspects of representing these different agencies was to meet the various characters behind the brands when they visited the UK. Unlike for example the French and Italian wine producers who seemed to have a rather lofty view of their importance in the wine world, those from the antipodes seemed much more grounded, with a sense of humour to boot which suited our culture!

No better examples of this were the owners of the Rutherglen Muscat wineries who came to visit Siegel's on various occasions. Colin Campbell I recall was very level-headed and approachable, quiet in comparison to some, thoughtful and friendly. At that time he was one of the few Rutherglen producers making table wine, a powerful heady 'Durif' which was fairly revolutionary back then.

I also remember when Norman Killeen came over. Preferring to be called "Norm" there was no pomp or ceremony; you sensed you were talking more to a 'farmer' of grapes who took pride in the products he produced rather than to an ostentatious winemaker.

However, of all the Rutherglen agencies Siegel's represented there was one person, in particular, I looked forward to meeting - Bill Chambers. The reputation of Bill's Liqueur Muscats were that they were some of the very best, and along with Mick Morris (whose wines were then being sold through Oddbins, but were not represented by Siegel's) probably the finest on the market. I remember we had samples of Bill's Old Liqueur Muscat's and Tokay's and these were stunning wines.

Bill's reputation was for intransigence, and no matter how many times Nigel might suggest a new label for his 'Rosewood' brand may help sales, he refused to budge.

The one time he did visit Siegel's when I was there it turned into a memorable occasion. He had come over from Australia with his son Stephen and the meeting would be held in the office around the large oval table. Both Nigel and John Boys sat down with Bill and Stephen, and I stood back in the doorway and just observed from there.

As it turned out this was an advantageous vantage point, as no sooner had all four sat down to talk than Stephen leapt in with the opening gambit and wanted to talk about 'Price!' As I stood there I could see Bill give his son a kick in the leg under the table as a remonstration for moving too fast! His inexperience had turned it into a tricky opener, but it made me smile, and I don't think either Nigel or John Boys were even aware of it!

MOVING ON

In the early months of 1991, I received a letter from Ivan Pascoe from Charing Cross hospital. He had been admitted for kidney failure but told me he was on the up. As I read through Ivan's letters now you realise the style very much reflects the person himself, warm and intelligent with an articulate humour. Sadly Ivan's recovery did not continue and he was to pass away a few months later.

My time in the wine trade in London was now drawing to a close as my family and I had been considering moving to the West Country for some time. I remember telling Nigel of the decision and as the time drew closer we informed the staff at Seppelt's in Australia. Both Freddie Choong and Maggie Hanratty were kind enough to recognise my small part in helping Seppelt's get off the ground in the UK, and I remember Nigel telling me I would be sorely missed.

In September 1991 I finally left Siegel's. I had worked with some fascinating characters in the trade and met so many fine people, and their memory is recorded here for posterity. I thank them all.

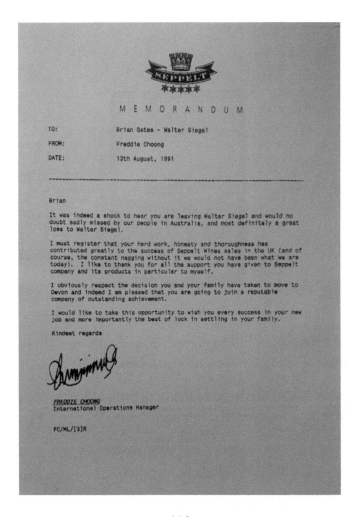

MEMORANDUM

TO: Brian Gates - Walter Siegel

FROM: Freddie Choong

DATE: 13th August, 1991

Brian

It was indeed a shock to hear you are leaving Walter Siegel and would no doubt sadly missed by our people in Australia, and most definitely a great loss to Walter Siegel.

I must register that your hard work, honesty and thoroughness has contributed greatly to the success of Seppelt Wines sales in the UK (and of course, the constant nagging without it we would not have been what we are today). I like to thank you for all the support you have given to Seppelt company and its products in particular to myself.

I obviously respect the decision you and your family have taken to move to Devon and indeed I am pleased that you are going to join a reputable company of outstanding achievement.

I would like to take this opportunity to wish you every success in your new job and more importantly the best of luck in settling in your family.

Kindest regards

FREDDIE CHOONG
International Operations Manager

FC/ML/[3]R

ON RECEIVING SAD NEWS

In 1993 whilst living in Devon I received a short note from Tommy Lambert the previous wine buyer at Cullen's. It came as a terrible shock and was very sad news which read as follows:

'Brian/

Met James last week.

He has Cancer. He stayed with me for one night I met his father mother brother + old mates.

He put on a good show but he is very ill!

Tommy'

Naturally, I would remember all the happy times working with James, and I knew he touched the lives of many others who knew him.

In more recent years it also occurred to me how little of James appears in a medium he would no doubt have enjoyed, the internet.

Having lost James in 1993, in 1994 I would also lose my mother. On passing this news on to Tommy Lambert who had known my mother well, I received a moving letter in response. A section of his letter also referred to the Cullen days and read as follows:

'I think I recommended you, knowing your understanding of wine, and willingness to progress.

You did a good job, especially after I retired, but unfortunately the family of the Rogers & Cullen could not cope with the Sainsbury Tesco's and others, and all you younger members lost your jobs and had to start again'.

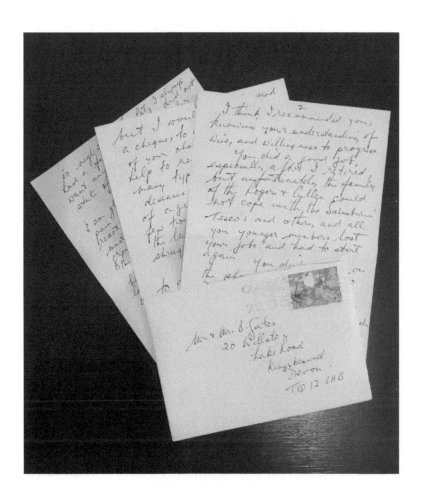

In early 2021, having decided to write this book, I decided to contact some of those in the wine media and trade who knew James from the past. I was unsure what sort of response I would get, but in nearly all instances everyone was more than willing to contribute their own unique memories of James to include in this work. I am grateful to all those who have contributed.

IN MEMORY OF JAMES ROGERS

'I first went on a Board of Trade Mission triannual to Australia in 1976 whilst with Walter Siegel's, but it was on my second trip in 1979 that I went to visit the Brown

Brothers in Milawa. They had a representative for their wines in the UK but he was doing very little with their products, so they asked me whether we would like to take on the agency.

The selling of Australian wines then was an unknown in the UK, and Brown Brothers only had four wines available, a Cabernet Sauvignon and Shiraz along with a Muscat dry and sweet. The stocks were sitting in St. Olave's bond, which at least allowed us to tentatively take stocks without too much of a commitment.

I first met James in the early 1980s; at that point in time he had just listed the New Zealand wine Cook's with Cullen's.

James had been to Australia and knew the wines so approached me about stocking Brown Brothers. He put together a mixed container of Brown Brothers, Hill Smith and Rosemount and was confident in the quality the wines possessed. This was the first tentative beginnings of the Australian wine revolution.

I remember James inviting me to the tasting room at Cullen's in Battersea to try some very fine reds in a blind tasting. Amongst the wines was a real 'find' a red wine from Bulgaria - I was very impressed with the quality'.

Nigel Blundell

'I first met James through Jane Hunt, my colleague in what was then a small importer of French wines based in Stockport, hardly the centre of British wine trade. It was apparent that he had an innate ability to taste without prejudice or prejudgment. He was able to marry the desire for real quality with an unerring commercial sense, enabling Cullens to stock exciting wines at affordable prices. More importantly though James was wonderfully kind and generous of spirit, treating everyone as an individual. I think often of him and miss his friendship'.

Paul Boutinot

'I think I first met James Rogers around 1987/88 when I started working with Paul Boutinot Wines. I don't recall exactly what the link was between Paul and James – most probably it was Nicolas Belfrage MW but it could have been Francis Murray, proprietor of London's 'Barnes Wine Shop' at the time. Nevertheless, the sure link with all these chaps was their fundamental and similar approach to wine – that a wine's quality and its saleability, regardless of price, were the all-important issues. All pioneered the philosophy that the intrinsic quality of any wine is in its taste and its appeal to a buyer/drinker. Some hugely expensive wines (due to fame!) do not always hold that intrinsic quality whilst many inexpensive and medium-priced wines may do and should not be ignored.

I happily subscribed to this philosophy having previously been shown a much similar view under the tutelage of my first wine mentor, Ted Hale MW, in earlier years at Harvey's of Bristol. James continually reinforced this approach, encouraging me in both the spheres of buying or selling wine. He always reminded me to ask: 'Do I like this wine, can I sell it, and can my company afford to buy it to sell it on?' – if the answer is 'yes' to all, then the green light is on!!

So, what more of James. I remember him especially for his enthusiasm, his energy, his 'joie di vivre' and his great sense of humour and all these with great happiness. But I also remember him for his car driving behaviour which was rather less to my appreciation. I really hate being a passenger and especially being driven very fast. In what year precisely I do not recall but it was arranged that James would be my 'chauffeur' to Vinexpo in Bordeaux. He collected me from my flat in Battersea and then I realised I was in for my personal journey from hell as we speeded down to the Dover. Of course, James was a hugely experienced driver and we made it safely to Bordeaux in record time with an overnight stop somewhere on the way in France. The only incident on the way was being stopped by the French Police for speeding....I suggested to James that he pretend he didn't speak a word of French. After he paid the considerable 'on the spot' fine for doing something like 160 kmph in a 90 kmph limit, he admitted to me that he didn't speak a word of French anyway!!!

Later on, in this memorable visit to Vinexpo, when a bunch of us were lodged at a 'gite' in the Entre Deux Mers, James, Robert Joseph and I went out for an evening meal consisting of a HUGE 'Assiette Fruits de Mers'. As anyone will know the ratio of food consumption to wine with such a dish when poking out morsels of shellfish over a long period of time is disproportionate. On the drive back to the gite, James tried to show it possible to drive standing up with the roof open. We arrived shrieking with laughter – and fortunately safely – to be met with a locked out Margaret Rand who was clearly 'not amused'.

Looking back, the one thing I feel so sad about is that James lived in a time when his homosexuality was something to be kept very private. I am sure few of his genuine wine-trade friends would have found this a concern, but he knew it just wasn't something the wider elements of the industry would have felt comfortable with. As the various infirmities relating to Aids got hold of his health, many of us did not realise what was going on but it did seem odd to me that he seemed to succumb to so many different health issues. It was easier to think cancer was the culprit as I think it suited him. I so wish many of us could have been more supportive in the knowledge that James had Aids and that he had a loving partner earlier in his decline but we understand he needed for this to be very private for this.

He was just another of those many whose lives were cut short by Aids before management of this horrid disease became controllable'.

Jane Hunt MW

'It was a Friday evening in 1984, and I'd just returned from a tiring trip, had enjoyed a couple of glasses of wine and was looking forward to a lie-in the next day. Then James rang. I didn't know him very well – we'd tasted together with Oz Clarke for his Sunday Express panel, but hadn't really had the chance to talk for long - so I was not expecting his invitation. "I've got a few wines to look at tomorrow. Do you fancy coming over to the Cullens offices to taste them with me?"

I imagined that he wanted to show off a few of his latest finds in the hope of my maybe mentioning them in *What? WINE*, the magazine I had launched the previous year and was then editing. But I was wrong. Walking into the building – "Mister James is upstairs" – I found him in a room standing beside a long parade of bottles. I can't remember if they were wrapped in foil or in bags, but their identities were well hidden and I'm sure there were 60 or more. This looked like hard work for a hungover Saturday morning.

"I do this every week" he explained. One of his team had the job of taking all the samples importers and agents had sent to Cullens, and camouflaging them alongside similar wines that were already on the shops' shelves. The task facing us was to taste them all, pick out the best and guess their retail price. Any newcomers that were better and more keenly priced than the incumbents stood a good chance of being listed.

But there was another little challenge. We had no idea of any of the regions or grapes. "If it doesn't taste like Chablis, I'm not buying it." He explained. And if a £1.79 Bulgarian Cabernet Sauvignon tastes like Bordeaux that would cost twice as much, of course I'll have it."

I can't remember what time we started this activity, but I do recall feeling like a carthorse in a race against a stallion. By the time I was taking my first sniff of the first wine, I'm sure he was spitting out number 10. Not only was he a phenomenally accurate taster, he was also ridiculously quick and competitive.

This also applied to other aspects of his life, including real tennis and the way he drove his professionally tuned VW Golf GTI.

A year or so after that early morning session, and after we'd both been members of the UK team of blind tasters that beat the US at an event in New York, I had another call from James. "Are you going to Vinexpo?" I replied that I'd been hoping to, but was struggling to find a hotel. "Don't worry" he said. "I'll sort it". A short while later he rang to say that one of his suppliers had found us a couple of rooms in a country inn, near their HQ, about an hour from Bordeaux. Politeness required us to visit the winery and attend a dinner with them after the drive from London – which we did at ridiculous speed. The brief walk-around at the winery included a classic moment when James looked up at a sizeable pipe and wondered aloud "How far *are* we from Narbonne?". Our host did indeed sell wine from the south, but I'm not sure that, as a Bordeaux-based business, he was entirely amused by the joke. This may have had some bearing on what happened a few hours later.

Following a lengthy dinner, Host said that he'd lead us to the village where we'd be staying. It was, he said, around half an hour's drive from the restaurant. He set off in his – then new-to-market – Audi Quattro and we followed at a normal speed. Then, the mood changed. He accelerated, and kept on doing so, and we kept up. Soon, we were heading round winding country roads, past a variety of warning signs, at 70 or faster. The Quattro's 4-wheel drive made it an ideal vehicle for this activity. James had to work a lot harder with the Golf but he clearly relished the challenge. I was unashamedly terrified.

After what seemed like several hours, but was probably a lot less than the predicted 30 minutes, we arrived safely at the auberge. We'd blown the exhaust.

The next day, I was with James when we visited Host's Vinexpo stand to thank him for dinner and to ask if he could recommend a good garage. The sight of the Frenchman commiserating politely while struggling to suppress the smile he hadn't given to James's quip about Narbonne, has stuck firmly in my mind. James was amused too, and I remember wondering if there were *any* challenge he'd ever decline'.

Robert Joseph

'Kaaayteee'

'Yes James'

'I will be there in half an hour. Get the samples ready.'

This was a regular occurrence in 1987-89 in the lauded independent wine merchant The Barnes Wine Shop run by Francis Murray. James Rogers was our wine consultant.

There would be a frenzied scramble for us keen novices (Matthew Jukes and Robin Davis) to wrap up the bottles in crisp racing green Barnes tissue paper and line them up. As many as 100 wines, 'Old World and New' would be assembled, samples eagerly submitted by importers desperate to get us to stock them.

I had joined the Barnes Wine Shop after completing an English degree at Cambridge Tech. The interview was tough, it was lunch. This was 1987 after all.

Within 25 minutes there would be a roar and a screech as James's black Peugeot 405 lurched to a halt outside the shop. 'Right team, remember the three golden rules: do you like the wine? if so how much would you pay for it and lastly how would you sell it to a customer?

We, (yes We) who had been in the wine business for a few months were being asked our opinion. I had been brought up with wine, my father loved the subject, and I bought Peter Dominics one litre bottle of French red and white at University. I might have even known that Burgundy was made from Chardonnay but that was it.

The golden rules have served me well. James gave me the confidence to trust my palate early on but train it by always blind tasting, keeping us analytical but also grounded and to always remember the customer. It also taught us to trust the taste and enjoyment rather than just what the label said – 'just because it says Sancerre on the label doesn't mean it a great wine'. He helped me get a job at Oddbins as Senior Buyer and then on to Bibendum and Enotria as Buying Director.

Golf - James loved golf (and Kummel). My parents lived about an hour from St Andrews and my father was a member of the R&A so we would often meet James in the Bollinger tent at the Open Championships. I am not sure who loved that the most, me or my father.

Speed – James loved speed. He did everything a breakneck pace but with precision. He raced to tastings in the afore mentioned black Peugeot and speed tasted with a ferociously accurate spit and analysis. Once sitting in a traffic jam on Battersea Bridge I recognised the familiar roar as the black boy racer overtook 6 cars on the wrong side of the road to jump the queue. It was James.

People – James had a wide and varied group of friends. One of them was Preston Rabl a bon viveur of great proportion. They were always up to no good at the races, on the golf course or round a lunch table. The camaraderie and fun that they had was infectious and I am sure rubbed off on me, Matthew and Robin. Wine should be fine but fun, it's just a drink after all.

And lastly Wine – Blind Tastings were the key with James. They taught us humility and made us concentrate and analyse to a much greater degree. Amongst many things that James adored was the 'Options' game and I particularly remember him wielding a large colourful French Country jug round the table at Sonnys restaurant (our local). The wine within turned out to be Mouton 1945.

I am indebted to James (and Francis Murray for giving me my first wine trade job) for his time, his teaching and his boundless appetite for fun'.

Katie Macaulay

'It's already three decades ago, and yet, if I read James's name, as I did when approached to write something about him, my mind immediately conjures up the sharpest of images...and I can't help smiling.

Sadly, I only got to know him at all well in the last couple of years of his life. In 1988 I left behind 10 years of a very privileged wine trade life as a buyer for a national company, both wholesale and retail. I wrote a business plan for an upmarket wine store and learning centre where franchisees could be trained. I needed a partner to identify the sites and train the new franchisees. Someone to be the face of the business; absolutely top of my list was James.

Anyone who had the connections to their organisation's buying power was naturally invited to all the big tastings in London, then centre of the wine world. Any buyer could easily turn down at least 50 wines tasted for a single one purchased. So, of course I'd enjoyed meeting James many, many times.

I'd always liked the simple logic of his decision-making process. He'd blind taste any sample submitted. If he liked it, he'd put a retail price on the wine based purely on how it presented itself in the glass. If he could make at least the full margin on it when he saw the cost, he bought it. Within a large company such as the one I worked for, decision making was rarely so clear cut, but I really admired the idea.

By the time I contacted him to discuss my idea, he was already putting the Barnes Wine Shop on the capital's map. Happily, he liked the plan, bought into it and came on board. And thus began the happy time of giving birth to the Fulham Road Wine Centre. We applied his logic to the wine buying; I dealt with the shopfitting and the sourcing. Together, we found our first shop manager, Neil Tully, who passed his MW while with us and remains a great friend to this day. James started to look for franchise sites although we knew we wouldn't be starting to commission them until well after we had at least 6 months of experience with the Wine Centre to show people.

As front man, James was invaluable. The wine trade press all adored him. He whistled off to a major weekly columnist's house armed with a serious (one of his favourite words) array of samples just before we opened and back came an article all about us the Saturday we opened. We found ourselves delivering cases of our chosen house Champagne as far away as Scotland.

And so it continued. Not a week went by without at least one really good piece of publicity, frequently in the national press about our Centre and its wines. We had a tasting bench in the shop and either James or I if we were there could guarantee that any member of the public who came and tasted 3 wines with us would leave the shop with something they loved. In my case, this was down to 18 years of massive amounts of tasting and learning what sold through the statistics. In James's case, it was genius and a natural empathy for how people felt about what their senses were telling them.

So our first 6 months went by. The trading followed the business plan, and then came the Autumn of 1989: Recession…unforeseen by the merchant banks or any of us. Franchising receded into the horizon and we started to do more wholesaling and a little consultancy to keep things afloat. James became a somewhat rarer sight. I couldn't say now exactly when it was borne in on us that he wasn't well, but, as he started to need regular bouts of debilitating chemotherapy, we saw less of him. Fortunately, he was able to get away for some very fine recuperation venues and we, of course were happy for him that he could manage these.

The major point that I have to make about this time though concerns how we reacted when we did see him. By this time there were several people working there. Without exception though, when he walked in, we all stopped what we were doing at turned to greet him, like iron filings to a magnet. Almost a whisper went round: " Oh James…!" Even the original Bond would have been a little jealous. It was, and remains in my mind, James's great gift to inspire anybody and to lighten their day and their horizons'.

Angela Muir MW

'James did everything at 100 miles per hour...not just driving. He tasted fast, he ate fast, he played golf fast!...like a jack in the box, always excited, always positive and always onto the next event.

People often ask me 'How did you get going, how did you build your palate?' and the answer is simple...tasting with James. I started with what I call an empty wine memory bank. In the early days at Barnes we were often tasting at least 150 wines per week, usually 'blind' so as to not have a prejudice before actually tasting the wine.

He had a great knack of being able to transfer what was in his brain having tasted a wine into words and he was so often spot on.

When one looks back on it we should all be grateful for him being one of the innovators in wines from Australia, New Zealand, the USA, Lebanon, Bulgaria and many more to reach the UK.

He died far too young but he certainly lived his too short a life to the full'.

Francis Murray

'It's strange to think of it now but a family-owned small grocery chain, W H Cullen, was one of the best places to buy wine in and around London in the late 1970s. This was entirely due to James Rogers, son of the owners who had joined the firm in 1971 after a brief spell trying to be an accountant.

Having been brought up by ultra-conventional parents in the leafiest of Surrey's commuter zone, he had presumably been exposed to the most traditional diet of red Bordeaux, white burgundy, sherry and port that dominated most British cellars at the time. But a bottle of 1964 Viña Ardanza Rioja opened his eyes to pastures new and from then on he saw it as his mission to educate Cullens' customers, and anyone else who would listen, to real wine value, wherever the wine came from.

When buying for the company, his admirable habit was to taste the wine blind and to try to put a price on it. He was the most open-minded taster I think I have ever come across and he introduced me to many a bargain. I see that there are non-fewer than five entries for Rogers, James I the index of my professional memoir, *Confessions of a Wine Lover* published in 1997. In the first one I remember our first tasting together, in the dusty corner of the firm's warehouse from which he operated. He served me wines from such exotic (then) places as Austria, Chile, Portugal and, his big new find, a wine labelled Cabernet Sauvignon from Bulgaria. Partly thanks to him – and to Tony Laithwaite of Direct Wines – Bulgarian Cabernet became the go-to wine for the British middle class in the late 1970s and early 1980s.

When we moved house in 2016 and I had to go through a large drawer-full of photographs from my professional life, there were several of me and James, together with the then editor of Decanter Tony Lord, tasting wine in incredibly small wine glasses wearing white coats, like judges in Australian wine shows. James was an early enthusiast for the best Australian wines.

I always remember a big contrast between how James presented his wine finds and how other wine merchants did. Whereas most of the latter gave the impression of pushing the wine at you, singing its praises the while. But tasting with James was more of a voyage of mutual discovery. You approached the wines as equals, and he didn't hesitate to volunteer any justified criticism.

I see that James was present the one time the late, great California winemaking guru André Tchelistcheff came to dinner with us in London – along with Hugh and Judy Johnson, Helen Thomson of O W Loeb and Sally Clarke of Clarke's restaurant.

Tchelistcheff treated us to a couple of bottles of historic Napa Valley Cabernet, a slightly tried 1916 Calwa and an absolutely magnificent 1943 Inglenook. But it would have been no revelation for James that California was capable of making some of the finest wines in the world.

My saddest memory of James is of going to see him in St Mary's hospital in Paddington en route to Oxford where I had to hand-deliver to OUP the million-word manuscript of the first edition of *The Oxford Companion to Wine* on a little stack of plastic disks. (This was the pre-internet age.) Within a week James had given up fighting the terrible disease that claimed his life at the end of 1993.

Soon afterwards I was honoured to be asked to speak at his moving memorial service in the journalists' church, St Bride's on Fleet Street. The church was packed to the rafters, so much loved and respected was this seminal force in UK wine. I can't help wondering what he would have made of the wine investment vogue that followed.

Nick and I subsequently had the pleasure of lunching at the Auberge du Vieux Puits in the Corbières hills with James's very different (solicitor) brother William and his wife Hilary together with food writer Simon Hopkinson. I could imagine that, had he been there James might have got a bit itchy during the many hours we spent at the table. He may well have taken off to discover some of the local wine domaines'.

Jancis Robinson MW

'I first met James over a drawn-out, rather boozy lunch arranged by a mutual friend, Mike Rayment, who knew us both quite well and who felt we shared a number of common ideas, attitudes and beliefs about the wonderful world of wine. At the time I was the Buying Director of Green's Ltd, a very traditional wine and cigar merchant located at the back of the Royal Exchange. I was half-way through my Master of Wine studies and was ready for a new challenge away from the often stuffy marketplace that was the City of London.

We got on famously and immediately, but, before I committed myself to such a serious career move, I wanted to experience James's personal touch around the tasting bench. I certainly had no cause to worry on that front, as he was not only a naturally gifted taster, but had a highly realistic commercial judgement. I was hooked, and was delighted to join the company to run and develop the W. H. Cullen Wine Club. Over the next few years, the Club grew from a few hundred members to over 4000.

That success was due in part to the wide range of wines we offered from a large number of countries, including some that were only then being discovered in the UK. Most of those – Bulgarian Cabernet Sauvignon for example – were chosen only if they passed the rigid 'Cullen's Taste Test'. This involved a number of sample bottles prepared for blind tasting by covering them with tin foil. We would taste each wine in order, making normal notes on such attributes as colour, aroma and flavour, and then, most importantly, state the retail price the wine could realistically command. Then, when the covers were off, the cost revealed, and our normal margin applied, if we could sell the wine at a price equal to or lower than our target price, it would go on our list. The wines we chose for Cullen's were there because they offered good <u>value</u> not because of their label. This unusual and brave approach to wine selection was but one of the things that made working with James an enjoyable and unique experience.

We invested a lot in developing good relationships with many wine writers both 'old school' – such as Pamela Van Dyke Price and Edmund Penning-Rowsell and newer, younger scribes like Jancis Robinson and Oz Clarke. These relationships were often built over lunch (after some serious tasting, of course.....) and I'll never forget the lunch we gave Edmund at the local Westminster College. He was used to fairly highbrow establishments and was visibly shocked when James and I walked him just down the road to the dining room of the college, where catering students learned how to cook and serve quality meals. An excellent three or four course lunch only cost a few pounds and, since the college did not have a licence, customers were encouraged to take their own wine, so, of course, we chilled some Bollinger, and decanted some fine red and a fabulous vintage port. Penning-Rowsell was stunned by the meal and the wine and promised never again to judge things purely by the surroundings!

The Wine Club attracted a wide range of customers, including such well-known actors as Leonard Rossiter and Colin Blakely and the Speaker of the House of Commons, Bernard Weatherill, who was a family friend of James. My first introduction to Mr Weatherill was dramatic, to say the least. James liked fast cars and his vehicle of choice during my time with Cullen's was a black VW Golf GTi, which was kept racing tuned by a mechanic in a Chelsea mews garage. In it, we travelled widely around central London and I don't think I ever saw James put money in a parking meter and, in fact, there almost always seemed to be a space that would appear just as we arrived. So, when James said we were going to have tea with Bernard Weatherill, it shouldn't have surprised me when this uncanny ability was put to use as he simply drove up to New Palace Yard and straight through to the inner courtyard of the Palace of Westminster and parked the Golf in the first available space! Now, this was in 1981, only two years after Airey Neave was killed there by a terrorist bomb, so neither should I have been surprised when we were accosted by a policeman who told us we shouldn't really be there, but - since we were visiting Mr Weatherill - they would allow it this time but never again!

In 1982, James and I, together with three others – Mike Rayment of Chateau Musar, Andy Henderson of Torres and Richard Goodman of Cook's New Zealand wines – took a stand at the Bristol Wine Fair to publicise the Wine Club and ended up getting involved in a venture none of us could have imagined at the outset. We set up the stand the day before the fair opened to the public and were advised by Mike that he'd invited a contact of his to join us for dinner that evening. That person happened to be the wonderful John Arlott and that evening proved to be memorable, to say the least. Regaled by many of John's stories and consuming far too much of our company's products, we found ourselves in a mood susceptible to any form of humour and, inspired by the collections of graffiti made popular by Nigel Rees, decided to begin our own collection of <u>wine</u> graffiti. The next day, having procured a blackboard from the organisers of the fair, we began to seek examples of amusing wine-based graffiti from the public. With the help of those wine lovers attending the fair, Radio Bristol who gave us good coverage, <u>The Times Diary</u> and Cullen's Wine Club Members, within a couple of months we had assembled enough material to design and have published <u>The Wine Graffiti Book</u>, with the cover executed by JAK, the famous cartoonist and with sketches inside by Frank Dickens ('Bristow'). Most of the proceeds were gifted to the Wine & Spirit Trades Benevolent Society.

Finally, in 1984, James was the second person (after my wife) to congratulate me on achieving the Master of Wine qualification. I can to this day remember sitting in James' office sharing a nice bottle of bubbly in celebration and I am certain that a good part of that success was thanks to working closely with James Rogers. He died far too young, but certainly managed to pack an exceptional amount into his life. I am grateful to have shared a part of it'.

Paul Tholen MW

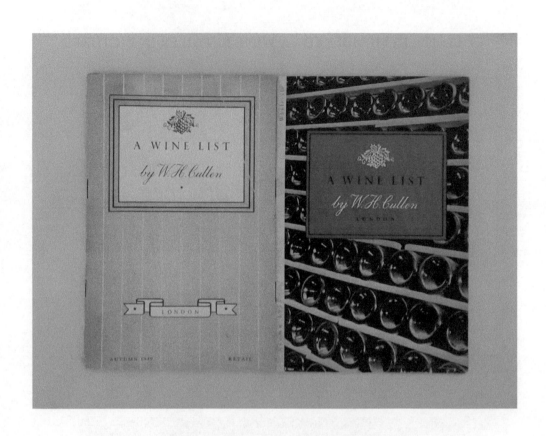

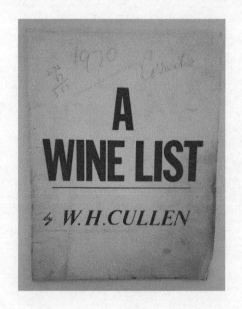

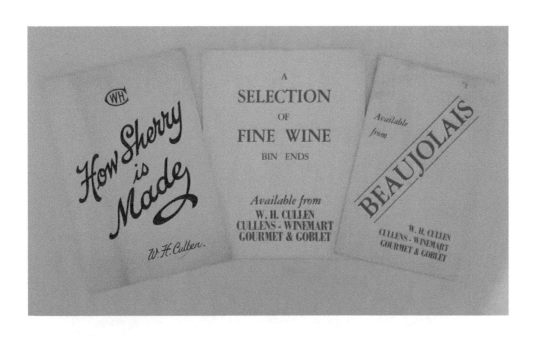

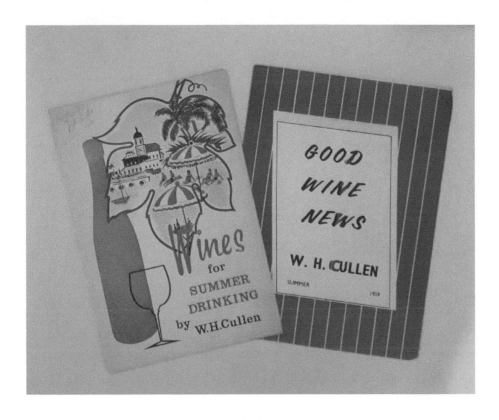

CULLEN'S AT WATERLOO ARCHES SE1 - IN PHOTOGRAPHS

Sadly, no internal pictures of the Cullen's wine warehouse in Battersea exist, but a selection of photographs taken for the 1953 wine list (with captions) do show the interior of the Cullen's Waterloo Arches, and give a very good insight into the workings in the cellars.

The main difference between what occurred here and Battersea was that by the early 1970s wine in casks was no longer being shipped over (except in the rare Offley port example) but in bulk transporters. In terms of the equipment shown in the pictures, corking machines, iron bins, and the roller track system (as seen on page 151) were exactly as used in Battersea. The rather grand-sounding 'hydro-electric bottle washing machine' however did not make it to Battersea after the Waterloo Arches were closed!

'A PART OF BULK WINE ARCHES SHOWING BURGUNDIES AND BORDEAUX WINES LAID UP ON SCANTLINGS TO REST AFTER BEING SHIPPED FROM FRANCE'.

'BOTTLING AND CORKING BURGUNDY'.

'THE BOTTLE-WASHING DEPARTMENT, SHOWING PART OF OUR LATEST HYDRO-ELECTRIC MACHINE'.

'A CORNER OF THE CELLAR SHOWING SOME BINS OF WINES, AND OUR HEAD
CELLARMAN WHO STARTED WITH US IN 1899'.

'BINS OF EMPTY BOTTLES STORED BEFORE BEING WASHED'.

'GENERAL VIEW OF THE ARCH STORING 'CASED' STOCK OF PROPRIETARY WINES AND SPIRITS'.

'SPIRIT VATS THAT HAVE STOOD ON THESE SAME SCANTLINGS EVER SINCE WATERLOO STATION WAS REBUILT IN 1911. IT IS HERE THAT WE BLEND OUR WHISKIES TO BOTTLE UNDER THE MCCALLUM MORE LABEL'.

'THE BEER ARCH. HERE WE BOTTLE GUINNESS AND STORE OTHER PROPRIETARY BEERS'.

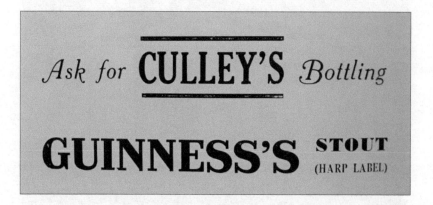

Ask for CULLEY'S Bottling

GUINNESS'S STOUT (HARP LABEL)

CULLEN'S ILLUSTRATIONS FROM THE EARLY 1900s

The earliest list that exists is from the early 1900s, but so poor is its condition it is purely in fragments. However, the artists' illustration's that have survived give a good representation of the cellars once again.

The most useful page in dating the list is perhaps that for Claret as it gives the vintage years against the wines, such as Chateau Latour Carnet 1895, Chateau Mouton Rothschild 1896, Chateau Pichon Longueville 1899 and Cos d'Estournel 1899. The captions below are as they appear in the list against the relative illustration.

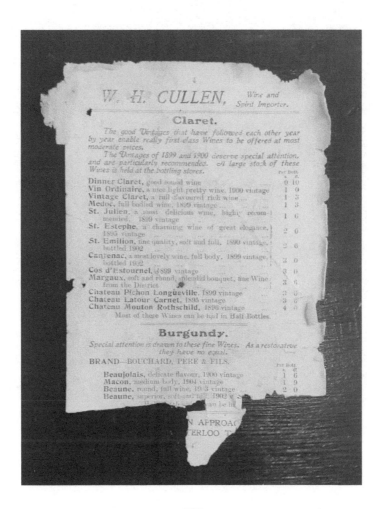

'THE CORNER VIEW OF THE BOTTLING DEPARTMENT represents an important feature in the Wine Stores. A competent staff of cellarmen bottle the whole of the Wines and Spirits at the Head Office Depot Waterloo Station, S.E., and stocks are then distributed to branches'

'The above view represents my Stock of Ports and Sherries in Casks ready for bottling'

'This is the BOTTLED PORT AND SHERRY CELLAR'.

LONG PAST MEMORIES - REVIVED

One aspect of writing this book was the realisation that many of those I had worked with in the past are no longer with us of course. But, it did not deter me from trying to find out if any of those I had worked with were still contactable today.

It is not often you get the opportunity to correspond with somebody you worked with when you were 19 years of age, but thankfully that has been the case with David Blaze! I also wanted to talk to Dave to put me straight on some aspects from the past for the book, and to fill out any background areas if possible.

I worked with Dave at Independent Bulk Wine Shippers (IBWS, which is covered in section 3) from 1977. On talking recently we laughed along at many of our joint memories from that time, but what of Dave's background in the trade, and that of Ron Haze?

Dave's experience in the trade was pretty extensive starting with Wine Cellar at Petts Wood in Kent from 1963, and joining O W Loeb's at Jermyn Street in London in 1965. From here he went to work for London Bridge Bonded Bottlers at Staines Street SE1 in 1970, and on to Lyons Wine Cellars in 1971. He then worked for Gustav Adolf Schmittschos before joining IBWS. After IBWS closed he went on to work for Unwins for 10 years.

I was curious to know if he had kept in contact with Tosh & Dave 'Senior' after they left IBWS, but sadly no.

On Ron Haze our MD from that time, he gave me the following information. He had originally started out at the railway arches at Chapman Street, E1 before moving to Carlisle Lane with IBWS. On its closure he started up again in arches elsewhere. He passed away eight years ago.

Thankfully Paul Tholen too from the Cullen days was good enough to answer my initial enquiry on James, and in his genial manner helped me to get the ball rolling.

It was also a pleasure to meet James Rogers's brother William and his wife Hilary for the first time at their home in May 2022.

William gave me some background information on James I was unaware of, his talent as a tennis player, and at 18 playing at the LSE, and an incident that occurred with one of his two other flatmates when he was studying to become an accountant. To his horror, one of them committed suicide, and James no longer wanted to pursue a career in this direction. Thankfully, as it would turn out for the world of wine...

I could also relay my experiences of working for Cullen's to William first-hand, and he enlightened me on other aspects from that time. I was very appreciative.

~~~~~~~~~~~~~~~~~~~~~~~~~~~~~~

PHOTOGRAPH CREDITS

Also showing original source material credits where applicable.

Nigel Blundell: 108, 109, 110, 119

Michael Chewter: 89, 90, 91, 92 both, 93 bottom

W.H. Cullen archive material: 53, 54 all, 82, 83, 142, 143, 144, 145, 146, 147, 148, 149, 150, 151, 152, 153, 154

Decanter Magazine: 100

Brian Gates: 12, 18, 20, 21, 25 bottom, 29 all, 30 both, 31 all, 36 both, 41, 45 all, 46 top, 48 top, 53, 54 all, 56, 57, 64 both, 67, 68 both, 81, 82, 83, 93 top, 96, 97, 98, 113 bottom

Tommy Lambert: 120, 121

Lyons Wine Cellars: 26

Angela Muir: 122

Francis Murray: 139 top, 140

Quiller Publishing: 139 bottom

Jancis Robinson: 138

James Rogers: 137, 138 top

William Rogers: 140 both, 141

Sogrape: 112, 113 top

Symington Family Estates: 7, 88, 94, 99

Unknown: 84 both, 85

Which? Wine Magazine: 115, 116 both

~~~~~~~~~~~~~~~~~~~~~~~~~~~~

INDEX

D

E

Ebury Wine Bar 87

Elizabeth Street, Belgravia 79, 87

F

Falklands War 70, 71

Fells, John 39

John E Fells & Sons Ltd 75, 80

Fiddament, Alan 72, 84

Franchette Argentinian red wine 70

G

Gates, Patricia "Pat" (mother) 11, 19, 42, 60, 63, 64, 74, 77, 79, 85, 121

Gough, Raymond "Ray" 79, 80, 85, 86, 87, 95, 101

Graham, Johnny & William 80

Gus, (employee Cullen's warehouse) 51, 52, 59, 63

H

Hanratty, Maggie (Seppelt's Export Co-ordinator) 107, 119

Harpers Wine & Spirit Gazette 74

Haze, Ronald "Ron"   24, 37, 39, 40, 156

Hop Exchange, Southwark   26

House of Commons   117, 136

Hunt, Jane   86, 102, 123

I

Independent Bulk Wine Shippers (IBWS)   22, 24, 25, 26, 27, 33, 36, 37, 38, 41, 42, 52, 156

Institute of Directors, Pall Mall   83, 84

J

Jameson Irish Whiskey (relabelling contract)   37

Joseph, Robert   102, 125

K

Killeen, Norman   118

Kopke Port Wines   28, 35, 36, 41

C.N. Kopke & Co Ltd   28, 33

BV - #0114 - 180523 - C0 - 246/189/10 - PB - 9600683000031 - None Lamination